NETWORKIN
COMMUNITY
PARTNERSHIP

D0893062

To Rachel and Phillip

Networking and Community Partnership

Second Edition

Steve Trevillion

Ashgate
ARENA

Aldershot • Brookfield USA • Singapore • Sydney

Published by
Ashgate Publishing Limited
Gower House
Croft Road
Aldershot
Hants GU11 3HR
England

Ashgate Publishing Company
Old Post Road
Brookfield
Vermont 05036
USA

British Library Cataloguing in Publication Data
Trevillion, Steve
  Networking and community partnership. – 2nd ed.
  1. Social networks   2. Human services   3. Community organization
  4. Social policy – Case studies
  I. Title   II. Caring in the community
  361.3

Library of Congress Cataloging-in-Publication Data
Trevillion, Steve.
  Networking and community partnership / Steve Trevillion. – 2nd ed.
    p.   cm
    ISBN 1-85742-426-3 (pb)
    1. Social service—Great Britain.   2. Community organization—Great Britain.   3. Social networks—Great Britain.   4. Social group work—Great Britain.   I. Trevillion, Steve. Caring in the community.   II. Title.
  HV245.T74   1999
  361.8'0941—dc21   98-52025
                                                                   CIP

ISBN 1 85742 426 3

Typeset by Manton Typesetters, 5–7 Eastfield Road, Louth, Lincs, LN11 7AJ, UK.

Printed and bound by Athenaeum Press, Ltd.,
Gateshead, Tyne & Wear.

Contents

List of figures   vii

Acknowledgements   ix

Introduction   1

1   Social welfare and social networks   15

2   Networking: a theory for practice   35

3   Assessment: a networking approach   53

4   Community brokers   71

5   Inter-agency networking   87

6   Care management revisited   103

7   Working together for empowerment   121

8   Networking with children and families   133

9   Teaching and learning   145

10 Conclusion   155

Bibliography   161

Index   173

List of figures

1.1   A social network   19

1.2   Primary and secondary 'stars'   23

1.3   A loose-knit network   25

1.4   A close-knit network   27

Acknowledgements

I would like to thank all those who took part in the research projects on which this book is based, including all the professionals, carers and service users who contributed to the West London Project, the social workers who took part in the North London Project, Elisabeth Weibahr and the other *kurators* at Danderyds Sjukhus who contributed so much to the Swedish Project, my colleagues Peter Beresford, Naseem Shah and Betula Nelson and my former colleagues Kirsty Woodward and David Green.

My renewed thanks are also due to all those who contributed to the first edition of this book, especially Andy Brown, Suneel Chadha, Clive Turner, Justine Pepperell and Alison Partridge.

Finally, I would like to thank Maurice Kogan and Linda Thomas for their help and support in the writing and rewriting of this book and all those who enabled me to focus on this work at a very difficult time in my own life.

Introduction

The first edition of this book was published in 1992 as *Caring in the Community: a networking approach to community partnership*. This edition has been thoroughly revised and rewritten in the light of recent research. The new title reflects a stronger emphasis on the concept of networking than was present in the initial text and the overall aims and objectives are:

- to develop a general theory of networking,
- to define the practice components of networking,
- to explore specific networking tasks and roles,
- to analyse the impact of networking on particular fields of social welfare practice, and
- to identify key issues for teaching and learning about networking.

The book has been written for a mixed readership and the hope is that welfare practitioners and their managers will find as much of value in it as students, academics and policy makers. The author is a former social worker but networking is an interdisciplinary field and what has been written is not just for social workers but also for community workers, health promoters, community psychiatric nurses and anyone else interested in networks and networking.

The term 'networking' has become almost as familiar to social services practitioners, managers and policy makers in the 1990s as the term 'genericism' was to the post-Seebohm generation in the 1970s. Thirty years ago, genericism was closely associated with the idea of a 'unified social services department': a large publicly owned and controlled organisation with a single director, directly accountable to local politicians and aiming to offer access through 'one door' to a wide range of in-house services for

1

individuals and families needing help (Seebohm Committee, 1968). In contrast, networking is closely associated with the development of a very different vision of social welfare.

In the 1990s, it is no longer assumed that social services departments can meet 'need' through the provision of a relatively standardised set of services. Instead, the solution to individual and family problems is increasingly seen as dependent on the linking together of a wide range of different kinds of organisations – private, public and voluntary – each providing some specialist contribution and the whole requiring coordination and strategic alliances rather than traditional management and administration. The term 'virtual organisation' has been coined to describe some of the more radical attempts to build new kinds of welfare structures betwixt and between conventional welfare institutions (Statham, 1996, p.10).

A number of specific changes have encouraged this trend. These include the National Health Service and Community Care Act (1990), especially perhaps the introduction of 'care management' with its emphasis on the coordination of complex 'care packages' and 'joint commissioning' based on the idea of a strategic partnership between health and social services (McBrien, 1996), the new emphasis on primary care teams (Jones, 1992) and the introduction of health and education 'action zones' (Peck and Poxton, 1998). Some of these changes have been driven forward by governments committed to market ideologies and various versions of communitarianism (Etzioni, 1995); some have been generated by grassroots social movements (Brandon, 1995).

All of these developments have been accompanied by endless calls for those involved with assessing need and planning or delivering services, whether for communities as a whole or for specific individuals, to network with one another outside conventional organisational structures and systems so as to develop new types of partnership transcending sectoral boundaries and linking planners, purchasers, providers and users of services with one another and with communities as a whole. So closely identified has networking become with this broad vision of partnership that it is impossible to discuss it in isolation from the emergence of that vision.

While the partnership concept was originally used in a limited way to indicate that 'clients are fellow citizens' (British Association of Social Workers, 1980) and therefore entitled to be treated with respect by professional social workers, in recent years it has become identified with the much bigger idea that social services themselves should be seen as a product of a wide-ranging social partnership (Etzioni, 1995; Hutton, 1997). As a result, what was once identified with particular areas of social policy such as child care and community care now seems to have permeated the fabric of policy making in local as well as central government. To take just one example of this, the London Borough of Croydon has described its anti-poverty strategy as one which is explicitly based on the partnership principle: 'To improve the quality of life and opportunities for groups and individuals across the Borough by working in partnership with other public bodies, the private sector, voluntary organisations, community groups and other agencies' (Croydon Strategic Projects, 1997).

This is not a purely local or national phenomenon. Within the broader European context, the 'New Community Partnership' designed to embrace local people, local government and local business in an integrated fashion (Macfarlane and Laville, 1992) is but one of the attempts currently being made to revive civil society and social solidarity in the European Union. But unless something is done to enable these ever more ambitious partnership structures to fulfil their promises of mutual understanding and joint decision making, there is a danger that the sheer complexity of roles, tasks and relationships characteristic of the new welfare partnerships, already exacerbated by the impact of globalisation and deregulation (Trevillion, 1996a, p.100), may lead only to higher levels of confusion, poorer decisions and a downward spiral in the level of service quality. It is here, where vision and rhetoric have to be translated into practice, that networking can be located. However, networking, like partnership, is not immune to the dangers of inflated expectations and so it is important to establish a reliable definition before going any further.

Problems of definition

Of genericism, it has been said that 'from the very beginning there was controversy as to what this term actually meant and what form its application in practice might take' (Challis, 1990, p.40). Unfortunately, much the same, it seems, could be said about networking. Some have suggested that networking is inextricably linked to the introduction of social care markets and the development of new kinds of relationships between organisations (Laming, 1989, p.19). Others have suggested that networking is a way of injecting more analytic rigor into 'post-Griffiths case management' (Sharkey, 1989, p.391) by taking into account issues such as size and density of social networks. On the other hand, Payne has argued that almost any kind of 'linking' work can be described as networking (Payne, 1993). At the same time, and under the influence of popular versions of management theory, networking has also become identified with the use of informal social contacts as a route to securing information, influence and career advancement.

While there is nothing wrong with the development of particular versions of any theory in order to suit particular circumstances or to solve particular problems, the sheer variety of ideas about networking and the vagueness of the ways in which these ideas have been expressed is a cause for concern. The history of social welfare is littered with ideas which were once fashionable but which were found wanting when hard questions were asked of them. The problems associated with defining 'genericism' contributed to its collapse in the face of demands for specialist expertise, and the claims of 'community social work' (Barclay, 1982) were made to look very shallow as soon as the concept of 'community' began to be subjected to critical scrutiny. Social welfare may now be organised on network principles, but this, in itself, is not a theory of networking. At best, it is one of the issues which such a theory needs to explain.

The first problem which arises is the need to ensure that any definition of networking is broad enough to encompass the diversity of networking practices without degenerating into vacuous generalisations about 'partnership' and 'community'. At the very least, any definition of networking has to be broad enough to include such activities as the chairing of network conferences, inter-agency networking, the coordination of complex support networks and the mobilisation of activist networks for campaign purposes without becoming meaningless.

A secondary problem is that many of the skills and practices associated with networking often resemble those associated with other well-established psychosocial theories, methods and techniques. For example, chairing a network conference involves assembling a particular network in one place at one time. Superficially, this appears to make it very difficult to clearly separate network conferencing from groupwork.

The solution to the problem of diversity is to build into any definition of networking the one feature which is not only shared by all the examples given but is also a key aspect of all the new welfare 'partnerships': boundaries and boundary crossing. These boundaries might reflect entrenched assumptions about the roles of service providers and service users or be more straightforwardly organisational or professional or, in the case of activist networks, a product of both geographical and social distance and the isolating effects of discrimination and disadvantage. Sometimes all these boundaries might be present simultaneously. Networking involves crossing boundaries like this by way of new patterns of linkage rather than seeking to dissolve or abolish the boundaries themselves.

While any social network can be described as 'a specific set of linkages' (Mitchell, 1969, p.2) those links which networkers seek to forge tend to have much stronger cross-boundary characteristics than those which tend to arise spontaneously between friends and families. This has implications for the kind of networks or 'sets' with which networking is concerned. Inasmuch as networking is concerned with cross-boundary linkages, it is also concerned with cross-boundary sets characterised by internal differentiation.

The second problem, the overlap between networking and other methods of psychosocial intervention, arises only if we seek to explain networking in terms of some essential and distinctive core of therapeutic techniques. Networking has much in common with community work, counselling and groupwork, but this does not make it the same as any or all of these. What makes networking distinctive is its concern with the building of patterns of social interaction which try to combine possibilities of collective action with respect for difference. This is inherent in the cross-boundary character of the 'sets' with which it is concerned. Any of these are characterised as much by their internal differences as by their commonalities and this preoccupation with the 'linkages' which manage the tension between difference and similarity remains, whether networkers make use of family systems techniques, groupwork or community development.

While attempts to manipulate social ties could be seen as amoral, the theory of networking which is developed in this book is based on the core values of choice, empowerment and partnership. These lie well within the mainstream of much of the thinking behind contemporary social welfare policy and practice. What is distinctive to networking is the way they permeate its most fundamental structural characteristics.

Almost every facet of current social policy embraces the concept of 'choice'. Even if this sometimes becomes almost facile, the concept of choice is rooted in a concern with the dignity and worth of individuals, regardless of their circumstances, age or level of disability (Wagner, 1988). While groups, organisations or even traditional communities can all deprive individuals of choice, networks tend to safeguard it. In part, this is because individuals actively choose to join social networks (Bott, 1971, p.222). But it is also because, in consequence, networks themselves are defined by the choices of those involved. Social networks grow, diminish or change as a result of the choices which are made and networking makes it possible for individuals and groups to have choices that would otherwise not exist by opening up new relationship opportunities.

'Empowerment' is an elusive concept (Baistow, 1995) but, if we assume that it consists of a mixture of access to information, access to practical and emotional support, an opportunity to define oneself rather than to be dependent on the identities imposed by others and active participation in decisions which affect one's life, then networking can be described as empowering. Having opted into a network, one can gain access to information, emotional and practical support and, in some circumstances at least, an opportunity to define oneself in new and more autonomous ways. Some networks can be made more 'inclusive' and other networks can be developed to challenge injustices or to demand new kinds of social rights. Fundamentally, networking is empowering because it enables individuals and groups to gain control over their environment.

The concept of 'partnership' has been heavily criticised (Morris, 1993). It is no panacea and can lead to attempts to substitute heady rhetoric for practical help. But as a value it is difficult to see how any social welfare practice can ignore it, if only because the 'ultimate moral basis' of citizenship is the web of reciprocal relationships – the community (Jordan, 1990, p.70). In that sense we are all partners, all the time. But partnership is more than this. It also expresses the important paradox that it is possible to come together with others while remaining different. Partnership of one kind or another is therefore integral to all the cross-boundary linkages with which networking is concerned.

Drawing together all these characteristics, it is possible to produce a working definition of networking:

> Networking is the development and/or maintenance of any set of cross-boundary linkages designed to promote choice and empowerment which enables its constituent individuals, groups or organisations to work with one another for common purposes without merging their identities.

Much of this book will be concerned with exploring this definition in more detail and analysing its implications in an attempt to develop a theory of networking.

Theory and research strategies

Networking can be called a 'theory' only insofar as it contains some models of and for practice. Model building in the social sciences is fraught with difficulty and controversy (Blaikie, 1993, pp.168–97) and practice theorists have the additional problem that they are frequently attempting, not to describe or explain some identifiable, pre-existing social phenomenon, but rather to develop a model of intervention which will enable skilled practitioners to help to solve social problems of one kind or another. They are concerned with generating knowledge of and for action and, in relation to networking, the epistemological requirements of these action models are particularly demanding.

Networking involves theorising or hypothesising about patterns of linkage, the meanings ascribed to the linkages by those involved and the engaged or participant position of the networker. This creates a situation in which it might appear that networking is drawn simultaneously towards 'retroductive research strategies' whereby models are developed to explain observed regularities, 'abductive research strategies' whereby accounts are based on the concepts of social actors and the various engaged or committed stances associated with feminism, and 'emancipatory research' (ibid., pp.162–97). In fact, networking is not particularly eclectic. It has a distinctive epistemology and ontology, but it is one which is characterised by a process of making connections between multiple viewpoints and perceptions.

As a practice theory, networking can be broadly conceived of in terms of social constructionism, in that it is focused on the way in which particular social realities are constructed by social actors through the interactive sequences in which they are involved. At the same time, and unlike what has been termed 'strict constructionism', networking theory is not purely relativistic (Sarbin and Kitsuse, 1995, pp.12–16). It adopts a 'contextual ontology' in which the analysis of the ways individuals experience and make sense of their interactions with others is based on the assumption that there is such a process of interaction going on.

Networking is also strongly reflexive. The research projects on which this book is based provided opportunities for discussion in which there was no attempt to privilege one truth as against another, only to require that some kind of consensus emerge. These group discussions approximated to the conditions of an 'ideal speech situation' of the kind associated with Critical Theory (Blaikie, 1993, p.213). The search for 'rational consensus' is a distinctive feature of the contextual constructionism of networking. Both as a theory and as a practice, it is associated with situations in which linked individuals and groups are asked to reflect upon their common sense constructions in the light of other 'contextual' information about their interactions and interdependencies. In that this creates numerous opportunities for positive feedback effects, networking could also be said to share aspects of the 'circular epistemology' characteristic of family therapy and other systems theories (Hoffman, 1981, pp.5–9).

Methodologies, research techniques and data sets

The raw material of networking is social interaction and this book draws heavily on those theories, methodologies and techniques associated with the analysis of social interaction and interdependency. While the evidence on which this book is based was gathered using a variety of different research methods, including action research and case studies, the consistent focus on data associated with social interaction has led to a bias towards those techniques which have been developed for the analysis of social networks. The relationship between social network analysis and networking is explored in detail in Chapters 1 and 2. Here, the aim is to examine the type of network evidence used in the book and, in particular, the relationship between research methodologies, techniques and data sets.

The book contains a number of distinct data sets associated with particular projects. There are 'action research' data drawn from the West London Project, British 'case study' material from the North London Project, 'ethnographic case study' material from Sweden and 'historical' data consisting of case material drawn from personal experience. What the data sets have in common is that they consist of accounts of social interaction.

The techniques employed to gather the data included diaries (Seed, 1990), exploratory semi-structured interviewing of individuals and groups (Glaser and Strauss, 1968), narrative accounts (Gergen, 1995) and network analysis (Scott, 1992). The techniques used to analyse the data included participatory group methods (Beresford and Trevillion, 1995), thematic analysis or 'qualitative content analysis' (Berelson, 1952, pp.114–34), network wheels (Scott, 1992), grid and group analysis (Douglas, 1973) and, in relation to the 'historical' material in particular, the testing of conjectural models.

All the data sets incorporate multiple perspectives and viewpoints, but they do so in rather different ways. The West London and Swedish Projects analysed or interpreted many of the data collectively in the participative context of 'ideal speech communities' (Habermas, 1972), allowing both for different interpretations and for attempts to transcend these differences. The North London Project relied more on a formal triangulation between different sources of data as a way of handling the question of 'difference'. Finally, the case notes contain alternative views about problems obtained from those directly involved.

The West London Project, 1992–3

Funded by the Central Council for Education and Training for Social Work, this project aimed to identify collaborative skills. It was directed jointly by Peter Beresford and myself and conducted in partnership with a local health authority and a local authority social services department. It brought together health and social work professionals, service users and carers specialising in mental health work and work with older people. Although the focus of the project was the development of a community care skills profile, it soon became clear that this profile had to be located within a broader concept of 'culture' and the secondary aim of the project was to identify the characteristics of this 'culture of collaboration'. Fieldwork began in the summer of 1992 and extended until early 1993. The first phase of the project consisted of exploratory workshops. These were then followed by a series of user and carer group meetings and a parallel process of work with health and social work practitioners and managers.

For four weeks the professionals kept a community care diary, originally piloted with social work students, in which they noted details of their interactions with others and the way they responded to particular situations. The diaries were then subjected to a thematic analysis and a series of prompts devised for a number of group discussions. From these discussions general issues were identified and brought to a final workshop session involving all research participants when the various service user and carer groups, together with the professionals, were able to work towards a consensus around the question of skills.

The results of this project were published as *Developing Skills for Community Care: A collaborative approach* (Beresford and Trevillion, 1995). As well as contributing to an understanding of collaborative skills, the project showed that it was possible to research patterns of social interaction in the context of the planning and delivery of community care services and to link network data with opportunities for reflection on networking practices. This led directly to the next project.

The North London Project, 1993–4

This project was conducted in a different part of London and was focused, not on skills, but rather on a comparison between two social work teams within the same local authority social services department. The aim was to develop an account of the extent to which the rhetoric of partnership and collaboration was accompanied by purposeful linking between these teams and other teams and organisations and also to discover whether networking activity was associated with the development of new roles. It was funded by the local authority in question and by development research money provided by the Higher Education Funding Council for England and Wales.

While the choice of the local authority was partly related to factors external to the research topic, such as common membership of a Diploma in Social Work training programme, it was also related to a shared interest in exploring the implications of cross-boundary working in the aftermath of the 1990 NHS and Community Care Act. The two teams were chosen specifically because of their declared interest in the implications of cross-boundary working. Some attempt to achieve continuity with the West London Project was made, in that one of the teams selected was a specialist mental health (MH) team. The other team was exclusively concerned with HIV. While this represented the inclusion of a new client group focus, the advantages of inter-team comparison and the opportunity to incorporate work in an area which was widely seen as in the vanguard of community care developments were seen as outweighing any potential methodological disadvantages.

Planning began in the autumn of 1993 and the fieldwork phase lasted from January to May 1994. The methodology was negotiated with the participants. Senior and team managers within the local authority expressed a clear preference for an approach based on interviews over and above what they saw as the potentially time-consuming nature of diary keeping and group meetings. But it was not only for this reason that a new methodology was employed. Unlike the West London Project, which brought together a range of individuals from different agencies and teams with service users and carers, the North London Project was essentially a 'case study' (Robson, 1993, p.5) but where it differed from orthodox case study work was in its definition of the 'phenomenon' or 'situation' as certain kinds of routine activity undertaken by team members. The focus was not on the team, itself, as in Goffman's classic study (Goffman, 1971, pp.83–108), but rather on the relationship between external interactions and team functioning.

To begin with, the two team leaders were interviewed. Team leaders were seen as occupying a strategic role in the new decentralised structures becoming commonplace within local authority social services (Challis, 1990) and the assumption was that the team leaders would be able to offer particular insights into the relationship between their teams and the wider organisation, although all of this evidence had to be framed or 'bracketed off' in terms of the likely impact of their role and status on their perceptions.

The next stage consisted of individual interviews with both sets of team members, based on a semi-structured schedule. The focus was on gathering qualitative and quantitative data on network interactions which could be analysed in terms of a network wheel (Scott, 1992). This part of the project was designed to elicit information about roles, concepts of 'team' and the characteristics of cross-boundary linkages.

The data on roles and role sets were gathered in an exploratory manner using the terms and categories used by the individual respondents. Each respondent was identified by a simple code, such as HIV1 or MH1. No attempt was made to standardise these role categories, partly because different members of a single team were involved in very different activities. However, the use of some terms as synonyms was generally obvious enough to permit some standardisation of analytic categories at a later stage. These classificatory data were then used to create a number of boxes which were then filled in with data about interpersonal interactions.

Having accomplished this, it then became possible to explore qualitatively the way in which role and activities were classified and to locate particular linkages within the framework of perceived roles, thereby creating a series of role-based network 'sets'. It also became possible to develop a quantitative model of the overall pattern of linkages or 'personal professional network' of each respondent by extracting cumulative data on particular individuals from the whole range of role boxes in which those specific individuals were located by the research participants. This, in turn, made it possible to compare and contrast 'personal professional networks' both within teams and between teams and to look for evidence of any shared or collective team networks and the kind of activities which might be helping to develop these.

Some of the results of this project were published in 'Talking about collaboration' (Trevillion, 1996a). As well as showing how different reality and rhetoric might be in the field of community care, the project also contributed some important insights to the overall programme of research on networking. These included raising awareness about the sheer complexity of roles and relationships in contemporary social welfare organisations, highlighting the problematic status of the team concept in the new welfare networks and emphasising the difficulties which might be encountered in trying to develop new strategic cross-boundary linking roles.

The Swedish Project, 1995–6

The aim of this project was to conduct exploratory research on collaboration/cooperation outside the UK as a pilot project for a broader comparative European study of this subject. While the aim was to use anthropological techniques in order to develop alternative conceptions of cross-boundary working, a central concern was with the way ideas about cooperation could be related to and made sense of in tandem with an exploration of patterns and modes of network interaction.

The modest amount of time and money at our disposal led us to focus on a model which could be described as a short-term/intensive ethnographic case study which had links with some of the participatory methods pioneered in applied anthropology/development studies and referred to there as Rapid Rural Appraisal (Cornwell, 1992, p.12). A relatively extended period of preparation led up to a short but intensive and highly structured four days of fieldwork in Stockholm with a group of HIV specialist *kurators* (medical social workers) in May 1996.

As part of the preparatory phase, the *kurators* were asked to complete summary diaries containing details of their movements and interactions. These diaries were then used to frame the areas for discussion and exploration during the fieldwork phase of the project.

The fieldwork techniques consisted of semi-structured group interviewing with the *kurators*, presentation and discussion of case narratives drawn from the *kurators'* own experiences and a group discussion with the *kurators* and members of their professional network. The project generated a body of material which was published as 'The Co-operation Concept in a Team of Swedish Social Workers' (Trevillion and Green, 1998). The major finding was that, while some of the same forces were evidently at work in both the UK and Sweden in relation to collaboration/cooperation, the models developed by teams in London and Stockholm were very different. In particular, the emphasis on teams and relationships in Stockholm differentiated the *kurators'* approach to cooperation from the more individualistic, instrumental and outcome-oriented approach to collaboration found in the London teams. The contribution of the project to the overall programme of work on networking lay principally in the way it suggested that it might be possible to map various approaches to inter-agency and interprofessional linking work in a comparative manner.

The case notes, 1980–86

Throughout the text, reference is made to specific cases or situations in which I have been involved either as a social worker or as a supervisor/line manager. Ethical and legal constraints preclude any direct use of original documentation, and names and other distinguishing details have been altered to preserve anonymity, but, as far as possible, the authenticity of these professional experiences has been preserved.

Some element of retrospective reorganisation of material is almost inevitable when trying to present personal experiences some years after the events described, but my justification for using this material in the book is twofold. The case notes predate the development of any theory of networking and are significant not only because they represent the raw material from which the theory developed but also because they have continued to offer me opportunities for testing and modifying concepts and models of networking.

With historical material of this kind, the process of testing models and hypotheses cannot be undertaken experimentally. What can be done, however, is to explore the material in a critical manner to see whether the model which best fits the situation being described is one consistent with the general theoretical position of networking and/or which suggests that the theory needs to be developed further. This is similar to Bernal's idea of 'plausibility' which he invokes as an alternative to positivistic conceptions of proof in historical enquiry (Bernal, 1991).

Organisation of the book

The layout of the book reflects the logic of the argument by moving from questions of general theory to specific practice implications. Chapters 1 and 2 are concerned with basic theory. Chapters 3, 4 and 5 explore assessment, brokerage and inter-agency work. Chapters 6, 7 and 8 look at the impact of networking on care management, empowerment and work with children and families. Chapter 9 considers the implications of a shift towards networking for the education and training of social welfare professionals, while Chapter 10 offers a brief conclusion.

1 Social welfare and social networks

People are hardly aware of the problem created by the possibility that hundreds, thousands, millions of people may have some relationship to each other and be dependent on each other, although this may well happen in the modern world. Despite this general lack of awareness, the wide span of dependencies and interdependencies which now bind people together are among the most elementary aspects of human life. (Elias, 1978, p.100)

Complexity

Modern social welfare has become increasingly 'complex' (Hall, 1995). Whether one looks at structures or systems, the picture is much the same. At the structural level, it has become apparent that even one of its sectors, such as the independent sector, may contain such a diverse set of organisations that it is impossible to generalise about it (Taylor et al., 1995). At the systemic level, the delivery of health and social care services is now characterised by unprecedented degrees of complexity associated with 'the varying roles, responsibilities, resources and traditions of the many agencies involved' (Gostick, 1997, p.193).

The implications for individuals working within these complex structures and systems are significant. The following portrait is based on an analysis of the social network of one of those who took part in the North London Project, a psychiatric social worker in a large teaching hospital:

She was part of a large group of social workers, some of whom she rarely saw because they spent much of their time elsewhere. Although she was employed by a local authority, she spent most of her working hours with health professionals who were directly responsible to a National Health Service Trust. Her main role was the 'resettlement' of those leaving hospital. She had links with a voluntary agency which was largely responsible for many of the practical tasks associated with the 'resettlement' process. She also had links with a group of Community Psychiatric Nurses, a specialist housing association, the staff of two local hostels and members of the local authority Housing Department.

Within the hospital, she had to maintain relationships with the interdisciplinary teams on a number of different wards and to cultivate relationships with consultant psychiatrists. Apart from these face-to-face contacts, she was constantly in telephone contact with a number of specialist advisory workers in the field of welfare rights, one of whom worked for the local authority, while others worked for a variety of voluntary organisations. She readily acknowledged that the success of her work depended more on informal processes and personal relationships than any formal organisational structures and, when asked to which 'team' she belonged, she found it very difficult to give a straightforward answer.

In this example the experience of complexity is associated with a high level of cross-boundary work, a diverse range of 'partners' and a multiplicity of team identities (Trevillion, 1996a, pp.98–9). This is not just a UK phenomenon. One *kurator* (hospital social worker) who took part in the Swedish Project spoke about the way in which her job had become less bureaucratic and predictable and more interesting and innovative, but also, at the same time, more anxiety provoking:

> because the security also made us a bit lazy and maybe we didn't use our heads in the way that we could, so what's happening is that we have to use our heads more, that we have to find other ways ... I think that in this country we are not adjusted to this yet. I think we are going to find another way of dealing with things. Today, we don't know where to go for the next step. We are rather insecure, I think.

While Sweden and the UK have different welfare systems and the specific problems posed by the move towards complexity may also be different, many of the new challenges faced by social welfare practitioners in both countries centre on the question of building and maintaining cross-boundary relationships in a context of change: challenges for which their own organisations may have few answers.

Traditional welfare organisations have a number of strengths. They provide those who work in them with a clear sense of role and task, decision making takes place within clear structures of accountability, and standardisation of services ensures both a broad public understanding of what the organisation does and a certain level of equity in terms of service provision. A defence could certainly be made of the postwar British National Health Service and the post-Seebohm local authority social services department on these kinds of grounds. But, although well adapted to a world of limited expectations and relative stability, these kinds of organisations have shown themselves to be poorly suited to the complexities of a new welfare environment characterised not only by markets and the drive towards social partnership but also by the effects of rapid social and economic change (Statham, 1996).

The social network concept

Although many claims have been made for the power of social networks to solve social problems (Speck and Attneave, 1973; Maguire, 1983), at root the social network concept is a way of understanding complexity. 'The concept of social network paves the way to an understanding of the linkages existing between different institutional spheres and between different systems of groups and categories' (Srinivas and Beteille, 1964, p.165). Because it encompasses complex patterns of interaction and multiple viewpoints or 'normative frameworks' (Mitchell, 1969, pp.47–9) the social network concept can help social welfare practitioners to make sense of their cross-boundary working environment. It has to be acknowledged, however, that the term 'network' can, itself, be confusing because it has a number of meanings.

The word can be used as a 'metaphor' to refer to any kind of general and unspecified interconnectedness in society (Mitchell, 1969, p.1). This can be helpful, if the aim is to simply emphasise the complexity of our interdependencies. But it can easily lead to a 'rose-tinted' view of reality (Bulmer, 1987, pp.137–8). The move away from 'community social work' to narrow specialism and market-driven forms of care management focusing on 'cost containment' (Phillipson, 1992, p.122) can, in part, be traced back to the disillusionment with the language of network and community which surfaced in the late 1980s and was associated with the celebration of individualism (Wilding, 1992, pp.10–11).

So as to avoid, once again, getting drawn into endless debates about 'community' or 'neighbourhood spirit' (Abrams, 1980), we should probably avoid using the term 'social network' as a metaphor altogether. There are a number of alternative approaches, all of which build on the original insight that it is possible to describe social life in terms of specific 'social fields' (Barnes, 1954, p.43). Mitchell defined a social network as 'a specific set of linkages among a defined set of persons' (Mitchell, 1969, p.2). More recently, it has been defined as a 'perspective' which 'encompasses theories, methods and applications that are expressed in terms of relational concepts or processes' (Wasserman and Faust, 1994, p.4) and which has four key elements:

- individual social actors are viewed as interdependent;
- linkages between social actors are seen to direct the flow of material and non-material resources;
- the network environment is seen in terms of opportunities and constraints on individual action;
- lasting patterns of relations can be thought of as structures.

One might want to add that relations between groups or organisations as well as between individuals can be modelled in network terms.

Many different kinds of social issues can be explored using social network perspectives. These range from studies of inequalities in resource distribution to explorations of patterns of influence. For those working in the social welfare field, the approach also offers important new insights into areas such as risk analysis. This can be illustrated through an example.

Figure 1.1 represents a 'social field', 'set' or 'network' of the kind described by Barnes, Mitchell and others. At first sight, it looks rather schematic and abstract. Nevertheless, it is possible to see that A, B, C, D, E, F, G and H are all interacting in a particular way with one another. C, for example is interacting with A, B, D and E but not with F, G and H. Moreover, A and B are interacting only with C and not with each other. F and C have no contact with each other but both have contact with E and D. As soon as we make the example less abstract, some of the advantages of the network perspective become more evident.

Let us suppose that the social field to which Figure 1.1 refers is an extended family network and that A, B, C, D, E, F, G and H are all separate households and that G is a nuclear family unit – the Godstones – consisting of Mr Godstone, his wife Jean Godstone and their daughter Emma Godstone. There are indications that Emma has been sexually abused by Mr Godstone. If there has been abuse then the relative isolation of the Godstone family might turn out to be a key factor in having enabled it to remain undetected.

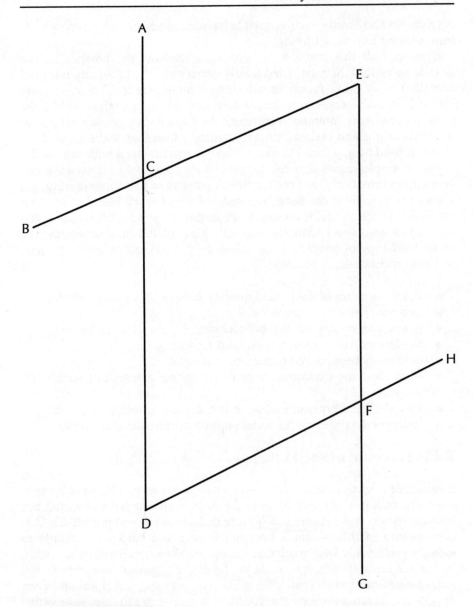

Figure 1.1   A social network

The only contact the family have with their relatives is Jean Godstone's regular trips to see her mother Louise Farmer (F in Figure 1.1). But Emma rarely accompanies her mother on these trips. There is no contact with neighbours and Emma's withdrawn behaviour at school has prevented her from making any close friends.

If we put all this together, it becomes clear how the position of the Godstones within their extended family network has reduced any informal surveillance by other family members to a minimum and has effectively blocked Emma's access to informal help and advice. In other words, the pattern of network interaction increases the exploitative patriarchal power of Mr Godstone and makes Emma extremely vulnerable, and this needs to be recognised by any social workers who become involved with the family.

This example shows that the process of mapping a social network can generate information about the relationship between risk, vulnerability and support which lie at the heart, not only of social work but also of other professions such as health visiting and community psychiatric nursing. The techniques associated with eliciting this kind of information about 'the social landscape of people's lives' (Seed, 1990, p.11) can be used by social welfare practitioners as follows:

- to take account of the impact of social change on social networks,
- to define network boundaries,
- to analyse 'connectedness' or 'density',
- to identify links between needs and resources,
- to identify brokers and brokerage networks,
- to analyse the exclusionary or empowering potential of social networks,
- to understand types of exchange and degrees of reciprocity, and
- to locate the potential for social support within social networks.

Taking account of social change

If social life in general and social welfare practice in particular have become more complex it is not only because the pace of change has quickened but because society has become much more differentiated and pluralistic. One consequence of this is that it becomes harder and harder for people to identify exclusively with particular closed social groups (Durkheim, 1933). In such a context, concepts such as 'family' or 'group' which presume shared norms and values can often seem anachronistic, unhelpful and even oppressive, because they are associated with an attempt to impose an artificial level of uniformity on a fluid and rapidly changing social situation. Unlike 'family', 'group' or 'system', the social network concept makes no assumptions and seeks to impose no particular order upon events. Rather, it simply describes what is, which may often be something very different from a closed group or conventional family unit: 'In network formation ...

only some, not all of the component individuals have social relationships with one another. In a network, the component external units do not make up a larger social whole; they are not surrounded by a common boundary' (Bott, 1957, pp.58–9). So the social network concept gives us a way of describing a whole range of relatively fluid and informal social phenomena (Srinivas and Beteille, 1964, p.166) which may be of great significance for those working in a rapidly changing society such as our own in which traditional institutions may no longer provide the frameworks within which people lead their lives.

The continuing movement away from traditional patterns of family life (Robertson-Elliot, 1986, pp.34–72) provides a good example of the way network analysis can help us to respond to change. The concept of 'the family' as an integrated social group may well be adequate for work with a relatively isolated nuclear family household, but if the parents divorce, remarry and form new 'reconstituted' families (ibid., pp.134–76), the resulting pattern of relationships will be a network rather than a group (Rands, 1988, p.128). Moreover, it may well be a network in which different individuals have very different relationships with one another.

The children of divorced parents may continue to see both of them, but the parents may cease to have any but the most minimal contact with each other. As a result, children and parents may have very different concepts of what constitutes their 'family'. If there were a social worker or health visitor involved, they would need to recognise that the family – at least as far as the children are concerned – is not a household (either of a traditional or reconstituted kind) but rather a network of relationships running across household boundaries.

Defining network boundaries

Any assessment which needs to develop a picture of the 'social environment' can make use of network analysis. However, one obvious problem is that social interaction has no beginning and no end. Social networks do not present themselves to us in a ready-made form. Rather, the 'social environment' has to be actively constructed by placing a particular boundary around the network (Wasserman and Faust, 1994, pp.30–31). In some situations, it may be more appropriate to start with a predefined 'set' or collectivity of some kind (Mayer, 1962), whereas in other cases we may want to start with one individual or group and work outwards (Mitchell, 1969), being prepared to define the boundary flexibly in terms of some measure of social distance rather than any shared characteristics.

Although community work aspires to community empowerment, in many cases the starting point is a problem defined by those living outside a particular geographical 'community' or 'community of interest'. From a social network perspective, this leads to a 'nominalist' or external definition of the boundary around a 'set' as opposed to a 'realist' or internal definition of that boundary (Laumann *et al.*, 1989). Sometimes the community work response to the nominalist/realist dilemma is to focus on specific 'communities of interest'. Again, from a social network perspective, this divides an original 'set' into a series of 'sub-sets' related to various 'minority' groups, for example sub-sets based on race, gender or employment status. But insofar as these categories continue to reflect external criteria rather than subjective perceptions, some problems are still likely to remain. The 'communities' which exist in the mind of a community worker may continue to correspond very inadequately to the reality of what has been called the 'subjective network' (Srinivas and Beteille, 1964, p.166) or the way in which individuals experience their own networks and may indeed seriously distort the nature of this experience.

Adopting a 'realist' approach generates other problems, many of them associated with the need to show that there is some connection between a particular network and its concerns, on the one hand, and a publicly recognised issue or problem, on the other. As a result of these difficulties, community workers often move between 'nominalist' and 'realist' boundaries in the way they define network and community.

When we are interested in the support which is available to particular individuals, we invariably focus on their 'personal network' (Mitchell, 1969). A care management assessment is a good example. The health of an elderly person might suddenly deteriorate, leading that person to request additional help from the local authority social services department. A care manager would only be able to make an assessment by interviewing both the client and those members of the personal network already actively involved, bearing in mind that the best way of supporting the client might be through supporting those members of the personal network acting as carers. But there are other people involved as well, and one of the difficulties with the personal network approach is that it is not immediately apparent how we distinguish between those we need to talk to and those whose views may be less relevant.

Although it is easy to begin exploring relationships using this approach, the sheer number of links that could be included in the network soon makes it unmanageable. One way forward is to distinguish between key relationships and those which are less significant, on the basis of how direct or indirect the interactions are (Barnes, 1969, pp.58–72). The full set of individuals linked directly to that person is the primary network or *primary star*. The full set of individuals linked to the primary star is the secondary network or *secondary star* and the full set of individuals linked to the sec-

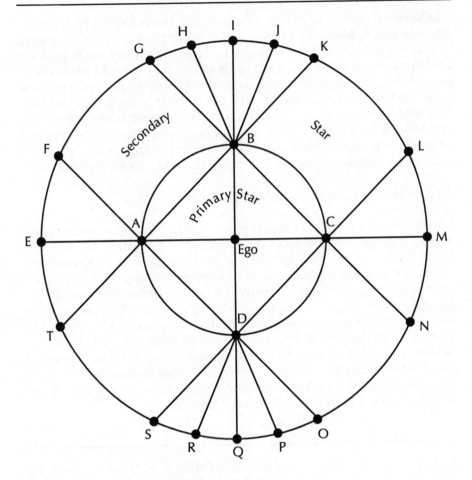

Figure 1.2   Primary and secondary 'stars'

ondary network is the *tertiary star*. The relevance of the primary star is obvious, but whether or not parts of the secondary star are relevant will depend on an analysis of the situation. In general, only researchers using snowball sampling techniques (Goodman, 1961) will be interested in all the links associated with all three 'stars'.

In the example, some parts of the secondary star (the carers network) might be significant because of their influence on the carers and their future actions. On the other hand, it seems safe to conclude that members of the tertiary star are so distant, both from the carers and from the person for whom they are caring, that they can be ignored. The relationship between primary and secondary stars is illustrated in Figure 1.2.

In network terms, the process of supporting carers focuses on the complex interplay between the primary and secondary stars. It may not always be easy to predict the effect of changes in the secondary star on the primary star. Moreover, another complication is that, while it might seem that a personal network approach avoids the problems of choosing between 'nominalist' and 'realist' definitions of 'sets' and 'sub-sets', this is only true with very simple networks. As soon as a care manager becomes interested in the *secondary star*, it is likely that the complexity of interaction will be such that he or she will want to start selecting particular patterns or sets of links to focus upon, based on some understanding of the key issues or problems.

Analysing 'connectedness' or 'density'

Unless there is a significant degree of interaction between people, we cannot say that they are 'partners'. The social network approach enables us to gauge the amount of 'interdependency' or 'connectedness' in a social field which is a measure of this basic element of partnership. 'Connectedness' (other authors use the term 'density') has been defined by Bott as 'the extent to which the people known by a family [or individual/group] know and meet one another independently of the family' (Bott, 1971, p.59). This enables us to distinguish between 'close-knit networks' and 'loose-knit' networks (ibid.). Figures 1.3 and 1.4 illustrate both types of network. A social network may be relatively 'loose-knit' simply because there has been no history of contact or communication. This is often the case with 'loose-knit' networks of professionals, as in this example.

In 1985 I was working as a senior social worker in South London. The departure of a colleague meant that I assumed responsibility for the supervision of a complex child care case and this, in turn, led to an invitation to a 'professionals meeting' at a nearby family centre which was to include educational psychologists, residential social workers, teachers and others, as well as myself and the social worker I was supervising.

Although it was a large family, my initial response to the sheer number and range of professionals present was one of surprise. It also quickly became obvious that those present barely knew one another and had little sense of working together to help a particular family, albeit one in which the children were separated from one another and/or their parents. Although many of the professionals had been working skilfully with particular members of the family for many years, some of them had never met before and had little idea of what others were doing or whether what they were doing was compatible with what was going on with other members of the family.

While it is possible to argue that good work was accomplished in this situation without the need for any improvement in patterns of professional communication, it was only after this meeting that a coherent therapeutic strategy began to emerge, partly as a result of pressure from myself and the social worker whom I was supervising. Perhaps even more significantly, it is hard to see how a network characterised by such poor levels of communi-

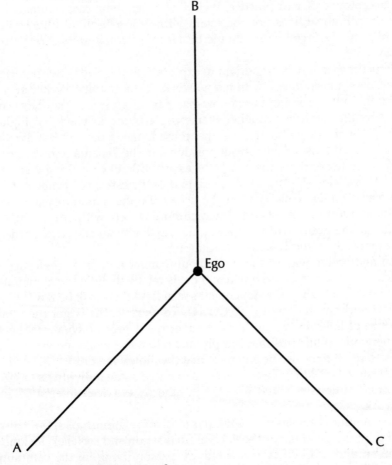

Figure 1.3   A loose-knit network

cation and coordination could have discharged its responsibilities effectively in relation to child protection.

Often clients find the lack of contact between different professionals quite baffling: 'Why don't you talk to one another?', they quite reasonably ask. The consequences of not 'talking to one another' vary from duplication of effort to dramatic and sometimes dangerous gaps in service provision. Moreover, only by reviewing with the service user the pattern of services as a whole can one get any idea of their impact on the life of the service user.

Sometimes too much 'connectedness' can be a problem, as with some residential homes, where the staff identify very strongly with the home and with each other and discourage contact between residents and outsiders. This is likely to reduce the capacity for healthy self-criticism and increase the acceptance of bad practice, including in extreme cases human rights abuses. Moreover, it is not consistent with 'normalisation' philosophy or the idea that residential care should be a form of 'community care' (Wagner, 1988).

Sometimes it may be important to explore the interplay between different levels of 'connectedness' within a network. A community worker may discover that people living in one low-rise part of an estate may have much more contact with one another than people living in blocks of high-rise flats. He or she may also discover that those living in the low-rise dwellings have secured most of the official positions on the Tenants Association and often seem to speak for the rest of the estate without consulting them. Here the relative 'close-knittedness' of one part of the estate is a problem for the estate as a whole, which can only be resolved if the community worker can enable the rest of the estate to interact more closely with one another and challenge the position of what amounts to a dominant clique by participating more fully in the Tenants Association.

An alternative way of thinking about 'connectedness' is the concept of 'holes' in the network mesh where there is relatively little social interaction going on. In a highly interdependent social field there will be few 'holes' in the network mesh (Barnes, 1954, p.44). Conversely, the larger the number and size of holes in the mesh, the smaller the degree of 'connectedness' in the network. While this may simply mean that the whole network is very 'loose-knit', it may also be apparent that the 'holes' are present in particular places only. This kind of analysis can show that some individuals or groups are only tenuously linked to what is otherwise a well integrated social network.

The presence of holes in a particular mesh of relationships should always alert us to the possibility of social marginalisation and social exclusion. So a 'hole' around a disabled or mentally ill person living 'in the community' may reflect the systematic rejection by that community of the individual

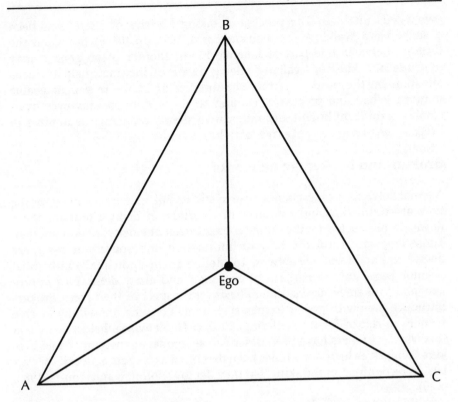

Figure 1.4   A close-knit network

concerned. On the other hand, lack of contact with neighbours may be freely chosen and reflect not social exclusion but something very different. Where a particular family chooses to distance itself from others in the street or neighbourhood because it sees itself as belonging to a higher social class, the hole in the network mesh around them is what they have created and is a measure of their ability to exercise social power.

From needs to resources

Meeting need is not always a matter of introducing new resources into a situation. It may be better to think sometimes about enabling individuals to gain access to resources which already exist. But in this connection it is useful to bear in mind the number of 'steps' or intermediaries required to get from one part of a network to another (Mitchell, 1969, pp.12–19). As the number of 'steps' increases, so too does social distance. Where there are too many 'steps' involved, it may not be realistic to expect people to meet their own needs unaided. The process of taking a series of 'steps' has been described as a 'walk' (Wasserman and Faust, 1994, pp.105–8), but where the distance between one part of a network and another is too great it may preclude any kind of 'walking'. Being aware of this may help to focus attention on the need to reduce the number of 'steps' to a manageable number. Where the process of gaining access to resources involves over-coming significant boundaries rather than simply reducing the number of 'steps', some form of 'brokerage' may be necessary.

Brokers and brokerage networks

A social network is an exchange system and its linkages are conduits for the flow of information and resources of all kinds. In many situations these flows are obstructed by the boundaries between one network and another. Those able to control the flow of information or resources across these boundaries and from one network to another are in a potentially influential position in relation to patterns of exchange, and many definitions of bro-kers and brokerage networks emphasise this aspect of their role. 'Brokers introduce men with power to men seeking its use who are willing to give favours in return for it' (Kettering, 1986, p.4). Networks held together in this way by brokers have been described as 'brokerage networks' and bro-kers themselves have sometimes been described as 'expert network special-ists' in recognition of the skills that they deploy (Rodman and Courts, 1983, p.20).

Within the social welfare field, the concept of 'brokerage' has been used to describe a range of professional or quasi-professional linking and coordi-nating activities such as service brokerage (Brandon, 1995) and ways of handling key worker responsibilities under the care programme approach (Dube, 1994). The emphasis here is less on power and control and more on the use of brokerage skills to enable information and practical help to flow across otherwise impenetrable barriers of bureaucracy. However, it would be a mistake to think that only professionals can be brokers.

Some brokers can be seen as 'gatekeepers' controlling access to a 'range' of network contacts. In these cases, establishing a relationship with them is vital (Henderson and Thomas, 1987, p.153). A social work team moving into a new patch office in an area traditionally suspicious of the local authority might begin to win acceptance by establishing links with key figures who could act as 'brokers'. Sometimes, these kind of links can have a more specific function, as well.

In 1982 I was a member of a social work team which wanted to offer advice, information and counselling services to homeless young people living in temporary accommodation. These young people were not willing to contact us directly. In the case of the older ones, this was based partly on lack of information about the services they might get from a social worker and also on a feeling that social workers would not understand or be sympathetic to their problems. In the case of the younger ones, this avoidance of social workers was additionally based on a fear that they might be forcibly sent home or 'taken into care' if they asked for help.

Faced with this problem, we decided to make use of our contacts with youth workers in a local 'drop in' centre and staff at a local hostel, asking them to disseminate information about services and encourage young people to make direct contact on the understanding that social workers would always seek to work with young people in trouble rather than force them to go home or to come into care, unless there was really no alternative. On the basis of this understanding the youth workers and hostel staff were willing to act as go-betweens, mediating between the team and local young people.

Looking back on this experience now, it seems to me that the social workers made use of a brokerage strategy, but did not themselves take on the brokerage role. Rather, by encouraging the drop-in staff to act as 'brokers', the social workers were able to ensure that channels of communication were opened up between the social work team and local young people.

Exclusionary and empowering networks

Analysis of the 'composition' (Rands, 1988, p.129) of a network sometimes reveals that certain categories of people are being excluded from it. To take a hypothetical example, a drop-in centre for unemployed people might decide to advertise itself by informal 'word of mouth', a method which might appear to have worked very well until the organisers realise that there are no black unemployed people using the centre. Given the high rates of local black unemployment, this can only be explained by the racism of the drop-in centre's informal network.

Similar implicit exclusionary devices, whether based on race, class or gender, are common, particularly in those networks where membership provides access to wealth, power or prestige. One might call such a network an *exclusionary network* because of its concern with narrowly defined membership criteria. The quintessential example of such an exclusionary network is the so-called 'old boy network' which operates to ensure that preferment in a whole range of situations goes to white, male, upper-class members of the network.

Empowering networks, like exclusionary networks, may be for certain sorts of people only, but there the similarity ends. A women's support network may exclude men in order to 'raise consciousness' and encourage assertiveness among its members. The exclusion of men is not an attempt to maintain privilege but, in contrast, an attempt to facilitate the kind of personal development which could lead to a challenge to the exclusionary practices associated with the 'old boy network', among others.

If we are serious about partnership and empowerment, we ourselves need to share power (Adams, 1990, pp.132–3), but this does not mean that empowerment is necessarily always a 'zero sum game'. A social network approach to the analysis of power and oppression focuses as much on ways of facilitating access to sources of power by reducing 'steps', creating 'walks' and removing dysfunctional boundaries as on the power differential between professionals and non-professionals.

Even amongst the relatively powerless, some may be more powerful than others, and one of the dangers confronting empowering networks of any kind is that energy which should be used challenging oppression can be used to maintain the position of a small clique. Where an ostensibly empowering network becomes dominated by a clique, it may resemble an exclusionary network and oppress those on whose behalf it may claim to speak. Professionals hoping to facilitate the development of empowering networks need to be aware of these issues because an empowering network should be empowering for everyone.

Creating new social pathways or 'walks' linking disadvantaged individuals to educational and vocational opportunities of various kinds can also be a way of developing networks of empowerment. A good example of this is the way in which social work education based in the universities can forge links with individuals and groups in disadvantaged and minority communities by setting up access courses in local colleges and linking up with key brokers capable of representing the university to these communities and these communities to the university. Brunel University has had such links for many years and it is obvious to all those involved that they help to enable members of some of the poorest and most disadvantaged groups in London not only to advance their own careers but also to act as role models for others who may follow in their footsteps.

Exchange and degrees of reciprocity

It has been suggested that 'mutual exchanges' lie at the heart of a healthy social network (Garbarino, 1986, p.35) and there are many examples of networks which do appear to function on the basis of reciprocity: for example, friendship networks. However, there are also many networks which are characterised by various degrees of 'directedness' or relative lack of reciprocity (Mitchell, 1969, pp.24–6) and complete reciprocity may not always be desirable if it prevents some people taking an initiative on behalf of others. The presence of 'natural neighbours' or 'help givers' on whom others are dependent appears, for example, to be crucial to the development of at least some neighbourhood networks (Collins and Pancoast, 1976, p.21).

But although 'directedness' may be of some use in the short term, in the long term it can lead to instability. 'Natural neighbours' may fall ill or move away, perhaps partly to escape the stress of taking on too much responsibility. Even where total reciprocity may not be a realistic aim, as when very dependent people are being cared for intensively by family friends or neighbours, opportunities for carers to meet and support one another (Trevillion, 1988, pp.302–7) should be explored as ways of strengthening these informal caring networks. Some element of reciprocity is essential to any partnership.

In practice, it is difficult objectively to evaluate the level of reciprocity in an exchange. Although some extraordinarily complicated statistical models have been developed to try to measure reciprocity, even the most sophisticated of these have been found to generate information which is potentially 'misleading' (Wasserman and Faust, 1994, pp.500–55). In most cases allowing the members of the network to evaluate their own exchanges is likely to be much more effective and reliable, simply because, when people do this, they are likely to take all aspects of their interactions into account and not just the more tangible ones. Therefore issues such as the extent to which all views are listened to or the extent to which everyone shares equally in decision making may be as important as the extent to which everyone is contributing equal amounts of time or practical assistance in determining whether people feel that they are in a genuine partnership with one another. Reciprocity may turn out to be inseparable from democracy.

The social support network

'Support' is one of those words which can be used too loosely. The main danger of this is that we can assume 'support' is present when it is not. Network analysis offers a way of thinking more precisely about 'social support', whether our focus is child care planning, care management or the care programme approach. In particular, it can prevent us from making hasty judgements about the 'supportiveness' or otherwise of relationships. While it is now widely accepted that all of us have a 'support system' which is embedded in our relationships (Caplan, 1974, pp.1–40), a social network perspective enables us to go further. Garbarino, for example, defines the social support network as 'a set of interconnected relationships among a group of people that provides enduring patterns of nurturance (in any or all forms) and provides contingent re-inforcement for efforts to cope with life on a day to day basis' (Garbarino, 1983, p.5). This suggests that support cannot easily be reduced to any one feature of a social network but is rather dependent on the interplay of all its characteristics. In particular, Garbarino draws our attention to the link between the support which is available to individuals and patterns of interaction.

More recently, Clare Wenger has tried to create a typology of social support networks based on the idea that 'support network type is highly predictive of outcomes in a wide range of areas of life' (Wenger, 1994, p.2). She has focused on older people but her typology is probably applicable much more widely. There is not the space here to do full justice to her work, but she argues quite convincingly that network types reflect different levels of involvement of people in the locality, with family and friends and with the wider community, and that network types are correlated to patterns of service requests (ibid., pp.3–4).Wenger's work shows conclusively that, when trying to analyse support, we need to look at the network, as a whole, rather than focusing on one or two 'supportive' relationships.

Two arguments against network analysis

Two problems emerge at this point, which need to be dealt with. One is of a general theoretical nature, the other relates more directly to using social network perspectives to solve practical problems. Without wishing to oversimplify a sophisticated technical argument, the theoretical objection to network analysis can be reduced to the following propositions: (1) the only genuine forms of network explanation are those which focus entirely on the connections between people and make no reference to the behaviour of individuals and by implication their values, internal motivations and conscious choices; and (2) genuine network explanations which meet the criteria outlined in the first proposition have little or no value because all the interesting or important issues can be described by making use of alternative explanations based on the behaviour of key social actors (Dowding, 1995).

Now the strength of the criticism contained in the second proposition is dependent on the truth of the first proposition. But, far from being a convincing picture of network analysis, the suggestion that authentic network explanations make no reference to individual social actors or effectively write people 'out of the script' is at odds with some of the most basic statements which have been made about social networks by those who invented the concept.

While it is true that the literature on social networks is full of technical jargon which uses terms like 'clusterability' (Wasserman and Faust, 1994, p.233), it is also notable for its concern with individuals as active agents. Bott, in particular, emphasised the importance of 'choice' in the construction of social networks (Bott, 1971, pp.103–222). Misunderstanding of this arises because network analysis does not recognise that there is an absolute distinction between the social and psychological domains. If the network is seen as the 'primary social world' of the individual (ibid., p.159), then it is through network experiences that the sense of self and the wider universe of meanings or 'cognitive social structure' (Wasserman and Faust, 1994, pp.51–2) is created. This does not mean that individuals are seen as automatons, but rather that their individuality is seen as embedded in social processes and in particular network processes.

It cannot be denied that some writers do seem to have fallen prey to an excessive 'formalism' (Dowding, 1995, p.158). They have lost touch with the fundamental objectives of the social network approach and have substituted technical expertise for the sociological imagination and, thereby, given network analysis a bad name. *But network analysis ought to be concerned with interdependency, interaction and social process and as such it should enable us to explore more, rather than less, fully the ways in which individuals and groups think about and act towards one another.*

The second problem can be summed up as follows. It may be possible to describe the interactions and interdependencies of individuals and groups by the use of various social network techniques. It may also be possible to show that a knowledge of social networks can help social welfare practitioners to be more effective. But it is not clear that an understanding of social networks necessarily leads to a distinctive networking practice. To make the leap from network analysis to networking requires a new kind of practice theory which draws upon social network principles but which can be framed in terms of actions and processes. This is the subject of the next chapter.

2 Networking: a theory for practice

Research, development and practice

Networking is part of the broader contemporary search for 'a culture in which common humanity and the instinct to collaborate are allowed to flower' (Hutton, 1997, p.65). This does not mean that all networks are necessarily a force for good, but, provided two important conditions are met, the process of establishing cross-boundary linkages is one of the ways in which the collaborative vision can be turned into a practical reality. The first of these conditions relates to values, the second to knowledge. Networking is a value-driven activity. What this means is that great care must be taken to ensure that any patterns of linkage which are actively encouraged or helped to grow are compatible with the principles of participation and power sharing underlying the concepts of 'collaboration' and 'stakeholding'. Armed with a few ideas about social networks and a commitment to building the 'New Jerusalem' of a 'stakeholding' society, it is easy to do more harm than good. Powerful cliques may become more powerful and manipulative individuals can inadvertently be presented with even more opportunities to promote their own interests. Networking must therefore also be a knowledge-driven activity.

Social welfare has seen more than its fair share of fads, fashions and ideologies masquerading as practices. All those involved, including service users, are by now rightly suspicious of the claims of any new practice to be able to deliver what it promises. It is time to spell out the relationship between research, development and practice in relation to networking.

The previous chapter focused on applied social network analysis. At its best, this 'incorporates an understanding of the client's world from the client's point of view' (Seed, 1990, p.9), but while networking is concerned with assessment, it is also concerned with intervention. It is much less concerned with mapping techniques than network analysis and its link with social network theory is of a different kind. Networkers see in network theory both a new language for thinking and talking about social interaction and a set of radical insights into how individuals and social groups can relate to one another outside conventional institutional structures, and networking emerges as a practice with five key characteristics which can be seen both as objectives and as processes:

- the restructuring of the interpersonal domain,
- building communities,
- promoting flexibility and informality,
- maximising communication possibilities, and
- mobilising action sets.

Each relates to a well-established feature of social networks and draws on this to generate models of practice rather in the way that groupwork theory was developed from an analysis of social groups (Sprott, 1958, pp.182–200). So these characteristics of networking are 'relational' in the same way that network analysis is 'relational' (Wasserman and Faust, 1994, p.6), but the shift from network analysis to networking generates a number of new research and development questions closely associated with these practice objectives.

- How can issues associated with meaning, identity and self-worth be addressed through social network interventions?
- What are 'communities' in the field of social welfare and how can they be developed or promoted through social network interventions?
- How can relatively rigid institutional/bureaucratic social welfare systems be made more flexible and informal through social network interventions?
- How do we analyse and go about maximising the potential for appropriate and effective communication in a social network?
- How do we mobilise and maintain 'action sets' in the field of social welfare?

This chapter will look, in turn, at each of the five key characteristics of networking and the associated research questions.

Restructuring the interpersonal domain

Social networks are the 'personal order of society' (Mitchell, 1969, p.10) and networking is relationship work. In the last resort, it is not agencies which interact with one another, but people representing agencies. But this kind of relationship work involves working in a systematic way with the connections between feelings about self and others and the characteristics of the particular social networks in which those feelings are embedded. In particular, the restructuring of the interpersonal domain involves *developing respectfulness, promoting reflexivity, encouraging reciprocity* and *enabling connectedness*. Each of these will be looked at, in turn.

Developing respectfulness

In the course of the West London Project, carers and service users were asked: What makes for collaboration and what are the key skills needed? The answer was lengthy and included many different types of personal qualities and skills. But the very first thing on the list was 'respect'. This was summed up by a service user: 'If they come into the house with a jumped up attitude, my back's up. If they talk to me like a person, I'm all right. I've been down that road and I don't like it. It's about respect' (Beresford and Trevillion, 1995, pp 115–16). 'The road' that is referred to here is not an isolated thoughtless comment or even a lack of sensitivity. It is a particular way of linking with someone which actively disempowers that person and makes it impossible to move on to establish any kind of partnership.

Much has been written on this subject from almost every angle, including that of the right of all disabled people, however 'different', to be valued for what they are (Morris, 1991). But the West London Project made it clear that, from a 'relational' perspective, the process of developing respectfulness involves actively circulating and making available to a network as a whole the multiplicity of views, opinions and potential contributions which are contained separately within its component units, without seeking to privilege professional perspectives. This is the 'road' of respect and it is intimately connected with reflexivity.

Promoting reflexivity

Any attempt to work directly with social interaction – the raw material of human interdependency – requires of us that we be able and willing to take account of the way in which we ourselves are perceived and related to in the way in which we work. Competence in this area of work involves that most difficult of all tasks, genuinely listening to and responding to what other people have to say. The West London Project emphasised the way in which working with others depends on a willingness to be 'open'.

As part of the project, nurses and social workers met in a series of discussion groups and several points relating to 'openness' quickly emerged. First it was emphasised by one of the groups that the way interprofessional relationships were handled at the assessment stage tended to shape the pattern of decision-making and if individuals were seen as having closed minds or fixed views it was extremely difficult to generate an atmosphere of collaboration. The group then went on to specifically connect this quality of 'openness' with the capacity of network participants to engage with one another and with the task.

It was as if the process of building links across professional and organisational boundaries could only take place if there was a collective letting go of fixed assumptions, a desire to listen to what others might say and a willingness to contemplate making changes in one's own practices. Another group picked up this theme and developed it further by suggesting that the process of achieving clarity about tasks and roles in a collaborative network could only be achieved if there was a 'blurring' of traditional roles.

An important part of being 'open' is being willing to take seriously other people's perceptions about you or your agency. This can be quite painful, but it is vital that the realities of the situation are acknowledged, however painful, uncomfortable or challenging and however much they may delay cherished policies and plans. Some of my own project/case notes demonstrate this quite vividly.

In 1982, I was working in a neighbourhood-based social work team heavily influenced by the then new ideas of community social work and community care. Having decided that it would be a good idea to emulate successes elsewhere in the country, and to establish teams of social workers and home helps working closely together, two of us arranged a meeting with the home care manager to discuss the idea. She also seemed keen and feeling decidedly optimistic we arranged to meet all the home helps working in our social work 'patch'. However, it soon became apparent that the meeting was not going according to plan. Nobody wanted to discuss ways of working more closely together. Rather, the meeting was used as an opportunity to vent years of pent up anger and frustration about their experiences with social workers. The level of distrust and suspicion in the room was so palpable that we had little choice but to recognise that we could not put any new service plans into operation until we had managed to resolve more fundamental problems.

If we had thought more deeply about the issues, we could have predicted that this might happen. We could then have focused less on defending ourselves and more on the important task of starting to build an atmosphere of 'openness'. In the event, the encounter forced us to think about how trust and credibility could be established and how we ourselves could act differently, in the future.

The fact that we had made the effort to come and talk to the home help group on their territory demonstrated 'respect' and, in spite of the initial hostility (or perhaps because of it), we were able to establish good working relationships characterised by what could be described as a 'blurring' of traditional roles and the development of new consultation and support structures which set in motion a process of change which started to influence others as well. Reflexivity is infectious. If one person starts to act in an open and reflexive manner, others may also become more open to personal and professional change.

Encouraging reciprocity and facilitating connectedness

The subjects of reciprocity and connectedness are best presented in tandem, as it is rarely possible to work with one without working with the other. The Swedish Project painted a vivid picture of a health and social care network referred to by the participants as the 'HIV World', which was characterised by a high level of informal socialising, a strong sense of a shared history and a quality of trust rooted in an expectation that one could ask for help on the assumption that at some future time one could also be asked to give something back. The following is an excerpt from a network meeting in which a brief dialogue takes place between a *kurator* (hospital social worker) and a representative of a voluntary organisation, followed by a statement about the 'HIV World' from another *kurator*.

Kurator 1: I know that I can trust her (pointing). I know that if I want something then I always get it. And I hope that's reciprocated.

Voluntary organisation representative: Yes.

Kurator 2: Maybe it is because the world of HIV care in Stockholm is rather small. We are not so many persons. We really know each other rather well, at least the people I have spoken to over the years.

> The second *kurator* then goes on to identify a potential problem with the pattern of connectedness and the basis on which reciprocal exchanges are organised within this rather circumscribed and close-knit 'social world':

I can understand that it is not very easy to come as a new person into this world because people know each other from many years back.

One only has to think, for example, of the problems posed for networks like the 'HIV World' by the demands of service user groups for full involvement, or the impact of those with a different cultural background or set of expectations about how people should relate to one another, to see that successful networking is often a delicate balancing act by which people are encouraged to develop existing relationships while being open also to new ones and by which isolation and fragmentation are avoided without taking away the possibility of articulating different kinds of perspectives.

Building communities

Collective identities

One of the difficulties posed by the concept of 'community' is that it tends to be opposed absolutely to both the values of individualism and the everyday social roles which tend to differentiate us from one another. So Plant, writing about community experiences, describes the process of joining a community as one by which people bring 'themselves', in the 'totality of their social roles' (Plant, 1974, p.16). But networkers are much more likely to be involved with the more ambiguous processes that take place in what could be called 'task communities'.

Any set of cross-boundary linkages in which the boundaries consist of more than simply geography or social distance can be thought of as a potential 'task community'. Members of a 'task community' may have little in common, other than a need to work with one another, but they still need to develop a sense of shared identity, however tentative, and the networker has to find ways of enabling a sense of collective identity to be constructed alongside other, often more powerful or more permanent, allegiances.

With interprofessional networks it is often necessary to encourage some letting go of traditional roles and relationships in order to build a 'task community'. The North London Project suggested that the difficulties the two social work teams had in this respect were associated with the absence of innovatory thinking about roles and tasks. Although there was plenty of evidence of multiple team identification linked to multiple role identification, there was no evidence for the development of new network-based roles such as brokerage, only a proliferation and fragmentation of more traditional roles (Trevillion, 1996a). However, this should not be taken as an argument for weak forms of professional identification. The evidence from the Swedish Project suggests that a strong sense of who one is and what one can contribute can actually help to promote a strong sense of collective identity between professionals.

Strong identities are not necessarily 'conservative' identities. Those of the professional workers in the North London Project appeared to be both weak and traditional and if the identities of the Swedish *kurators* were robust it was because they had been developed in the context of an overall vision of how the network could contribute to the care and support of those living with and affected by HIV in Stockholm. They were not the result of trying to defend traditional claims to expertise (Trevillion and Green, 1998, p.115). Sometimes, paradoxically, it is the effort to resolve conflicts and difference which can promote shared identities.

In the course of the West London Project, the interprofessional discussion groups explored the relationship between conflict and collaboration. One group came to the conclusion that making potential conflicts explicit at an early stage made it more likely that there would be fewer conflicts later on. Another group took this further and argued that 'honesty' was an essential basis for any partnership and that any honest relationship had to acknowledge potential conflict. It was pointed out that, when a network gets 'stuck' in its decision making, it is frequently because of unacknowledged conflict and that finding ways of helping people to own up to their conflicts and differences might help the network to move on to more open and constructive debate. The same group suggested that certain conflicts, although they might originate between two individuals or organisations, should be regarded as the business of a whole network and it was apparent that this group saw dealing as a network with a network problem as a way of generating a sense of collective identity. The discussion indicated these 'network conflicts' were likely to be connected with issues associated with core values such as 'racial equality'.

It is not easy, however for networks to tackle issues collectively and, while a third discussion group had no difficulty in agreeing to the principle, its members were uneasy about how they would actually put the principle into practice.

Empowerment

Health and social work practitioners are often very unclear about the meaning of the term 'empowerment' and how it influences their practice. This was the subject the interprofessional groups in the West London Project found it most difficult to discuss (Beresford and Trevillion, 1995, pp.57–8). In part this may be because it has often been assumed that empowerment consists of simply letting relatively powerless service users and carers make decisions on their own. But this is to mistake cause and effect. It is not the absence of 'disabling professionals' which generates 'enabling and empowerment' (Hadley *et al.*, 1987, p.10). On the contrary, simply leaving service users to make their own decisions unaided may be actively disempowering, unless people already have access to all the information they need and have developed a high level of self-confidence. It may be more appropriate to think of empowerment in terms of opportunities for participation. In the West London Project, the topic of empowerment only came alive when the groups discussed particular participatory strategies:

> A social worker described a practice of holding network conferences in the home of the service user rather than in an office and in this way symbolically giving some power back to them. All agreed that inviting service users and carers to attend was clearly not enough. People needed to be enabled to participate fully and if necessary to challenge the views of professionals there and then. (Beresford and Trevillion, 1995, p.63)

There are many different forms of empowerment, but building a 'task community' implies some move towards shared 'ownership' of meetings and decisions.

Enabling mutual support

'Mutual aid' or mutual support lies at the heart of any community process (Hadley *et al.*, 1987, p.11). In any community partnership members need to be able turn to one another for help and support. 'Task communities' face particular problems in relation to this. Care management networks may include a number of different carers who may not have had any experience of mutual support. Moreover, the presence of a number of different professionals in the network may also make it very difficult to expect the network to function automatically as a 'social support network'.

During the 1980s I was involved with a large number of network conferences which led me to conclude that the process of building a support system is intimately connected with the practical business of sharing responsibility and the symbolic activity of sitting down with other people as a new kind of collective entity with a shared identity and shared aims. The following which I wrote at the end of this period focuses on carers, but could apply equally to isolated professionals or home helps and sums up these links between community support and community identity in what I would now call a 'task community':

> Loss of self-esteem is linked to an overwhelming and undifferentiated sense of responsibility amongst carers. The isolation of carers and the ambivalent support available to them can be counteracted by the physical structure of a network conference. Seated in a circle, perhaps for the first time, the caring network is made visible to itself as a group of people each with a contribution to make. Within the problem solving context of the conference carers can identify and negotiate appropriate, limited and complementary roles. As these roles become more clearly defined the conference becomes more interdependent and more aware of its common boundary and purpose. In turn, this growing awareness helps individuals to internalise a sense of their role as carers and to resist feelings of total responsibility and powerlessness. (Trevillion, 1988, p.303)

Overall, enabling task communities to evolve consists of enabling people to feel a part of something positive and empowering with which they can identify, through which they feel they can enhance their own choices and the choices available to others and by which they can feel supported or offer support to others.

Promoting flexibility and informality

Conventionally, networks have been classified as belonging to either 'informal' or 'formal' types (Barclay, 1982, p.xiii) with the possibility of a third mixed or 'interwoven' type combining lay and professional care (Bayley, 1978, p.31). But all community partnerships need to be informal even if they only involve other agencies or other professionals and we can help to promote informality by our own attitudes.

When I was a senior social worker in South London I had responsibility for a case involving two children who were at risk of sexual abuse. After realising that my own child protection responsibilities and the probation service's befriending and after-care responsibilities overlapped in the area of marital counselling, I undertook several joint visits with a female probation officer to help the parents talk through their relationship with one another and whether or not they wanted it to continue – an informal conciliation service.

Institutionalised and routinised responses to client need, in which every agency focuses on its own conception of its responsibilities, allow certain unpopular tasks to be avoided by assuming that someone else will do them. As soon as professionals start relating to each other across institutional boundaries, it becomes much more difficult to avoid shared responsibility and professional roles have to be adapted in a much more thoroughgoing fashion to the task. By seizing opportunities for collaborative work, we put ourselves and others in the position of having to negotiate roles in the context of a particular piece of work. In doing so, we set ourselves the kind of challenge which is likely to stimulate creativity in ourselves and in our partners and lead to a greater collective 'ownership' of the task.

In these and other ways, networking can build on and develop the potential for informality implicit in any social network and informality can also be linked to empowerment. The Swedish Project showed how an informal style of work can be seen as part of a strategy for 'opening up' the social structure by making social institutions more responsive to relatively powerless individuals and groups (Trevillion and Green, 1998, p.118).

Maximising communication possibilities

Communication networks

A communication network is best seen as a pattern of linkages which promotes information flows. It can be a way of translating an abstract right to information into something real and practically useful. In the UK, for example, the 1989 Children Act makes it obligatory for social workers to provide more information than ever before to children and families. But such is the complexity of some of this information that it is only likely to be effectively transmitted if all those concerned with caring for children cooperate with one another to create the kind of linkages which enable people to listen to one another. Only when such an atmosphere is created can we say that a communication network exists. A communication network can, however, do more than this. It can convey requests for help and offers of help from 'person to person' (Srinivas and Beteille, 1964, p.168) thereby forming an essential part of the structure of mutual support.

Working with closed and open circuits

Communication networks exist along a continuum from relatively 'closed circuits' to relatively 'open circuits' (Srinivas and Beteille, 1964, p.167). All patterns of network communication have their advantages and disadvantages. In encouraging certain patterns of communication to evolve, networkers always need to bear in mind the purpose of the partnership.

Closed-circuit partnerships are able to transmit information to every part of the network quite speedily because the high level of 'connectedness' ensures that individuals probably hear the message from several different people simultaneously. At the same time, the wide range of transmitters should act as a self-correcting device ensuring a minimum of distortion in the message. If distortions do occur, it may be relatively easy to 'broadcast' new 'correct' versions of the message. In the case of a communication network focused on a child 'in need', it is likely that a 'close-knit' and closed circuit of communication would best serve the interests of the child and those of the partnership as a whole, enabling the social worker to ensure that parents and others do not miss out on key bits of information.

A closed circuit of communication may also be a very helpful way of establishing a shared awareness of neighbourhood issues. This is not only relevant for social workers or community workers. It has been suggested, for example, that health visitors wanting to know what is going on in their local areas should speak to as many people as possible by 'dropping in' on other agencies, attending community forums, inviting people for lunch and so on (Drennan, 1988, pp.114–17).

Where confidentiality is an issue, for example when a person has an HIV diagnosis, or where someone has disclosed a history of sexual abuse, communication should always be organised on closed-circuit principles amd governed by clear network agreements about the flow of sensitive information.

Messages passed through an open circuit are likely to be broadcast more quickly and more widely than messages passed through a closed circuit. Open circuits are more appropriate where the aim is to spread a message to as many people as possible. An example of networking to create such an open circuit of communication is the work done by those working in community health education (Gaitley and Seed, 1989, pp.19–27). Rather than focusing on developing a tightly interwoven partnership, community health educators try to forge links with a wide range of individuals and groups. In this way, not only is the health message transmitted widely, it is also varied to suit the needs of different networks.

Community workers have sought to disseminate information by direct 'street' contact with drug users in the hope that at least some of them in turn will pass on advice to other drug users. Efforts have also been made both in Glasgow and in London to reach out to resistant heterosexual networks by making information available at football matches and again hoping that the staff and supporters networks will act as a transmission system for health advice.

I attended two such events at the Queens Park Rangers stadium in London in 1994 and 1997 and also spoke to one of the community workers responsible for organising the liaison between the football club and the local authority social services department community health teams. What was noticeable about both these events was the use of a wide range of different forms of communication, all focusing on the same kind of safe sex message, from stalls and stickers to broadcasts over the loudspeaker system at half-time and the use of photographs, newspaper articles and so on, as ways of following up and reinforcing the message in the weeks after the football match. As the community worker made clear to me, the success of ventures like this depends on the building of a strong partnership between supporters clubs, football club directors, councillors and local authority staff.

One feature of all these community health education strategies is that they attempt to use informal networks as channels of communication instead of the advertising campaigns which often seem to create more problems than they solve (Wiseman, 1989, pp.211–12).

Managing the messages

The identity of the initial 'transmitter' – the point at which the message enters the 'communication network' – can be of considerable importance. If he or she is relatively peripheral, having only a few links to other members of the network, it may take a long time for the message to circulate. It may even get lost altogether. If, on the other hand, a message enters the network through a 'central figure' (Collins and Pancoast, 1976, p.21), the message may circulate much more quickly and effectively, as the following example drawn from my experiences as a social worker in South London demonstrates.

Responding to a request for a support group for all those involved in visiting elderly people on a local council estate, I called a meeting of these 'good neighbours'. I assumed that the best person to 'spread the word' about this was the chair of the tenants association who I knew visited some elderly people herself. I could not have been more mistaken. On the day of the meeting, very few people were present. The TA chair in fact knew only one other 'good neighbour' and was not the best person to ask. After the meeting I discovered that one of the social services department's own home helps who lived locally knew most of those involved in the visiting scheme and, when she was asked to encourage people to come to the next meeting, most of them duly turned up.

Networks tend to spread rather than direct information. Nevertheless, provided the number of intermediaries is kept to a minimum, messages can be passed through a network to particular individuals.

On one occasion, I urgently needed to speak to the mother of a child in care who had been avoiding contact with both the child and myself. As a last resort, I decided to try to convey the need for a meeting through an intermediary, the child's grandmother. Although attempts to make direct contact had failed, I reasoned that the grandmother might reinforce rather than simply pass on the message. The strategy worked on that occasion, although it subsequently failed.

Looking back on this now, it seems likely that the first attempt worked only because of the relationship that existed between the grandmother and the mother of the child. When that relationship deteriorated, the strategy became useless.

Information is power

Communication networks are rarely homogeneous. There are always features which differentiate one bit of the network from another. In particular, whether or not one has access to 'gossip' may indicate whether one is a network insider or a network outsider (Epstein, 1969, pp.121–5). Although a social network may disseminate relatively neutral information quite widely, the really important bits of information may only circulate within a small 'inner circle'. This often seems to happen in those 'interwoven' networks of social care in which professionals, volunteers, relatives and others try to collaborate with one another to help a particular individual. This is a kind of professional 'gossiping network': a clique set apart by access to a set of private understandings from which clients, carers and others are excluded. This type of situation makes a nonsense of any talk of empowerment and yet, because the power of the professionals is so dependent on the control of information, securing an agreement to spread information more widely can be very empowering.

Communication patterns can reveal themselves in a variety of ways and network analysis can help us to understand the clues which are offered to us and lay the foundations for communication networking. A community partnership is often only as effective as its communication network. There is no one ideal pattern of communication and both 'open circuits' and 'closed circuits' have their place. But it is important that we are able to facilitate the pattern of communication that is most appropriate for a particular community partnership and that we ourselves understand how to link up with and communicate along existing channels.

What must be emphasised, however, is that communication does not exist in a vacuum. Communication networking is as much about building trust and credibility and challenging the control of information by powerful cliques and groupings as it is about any 'technical' processes.

Mobilising action sets

An ability to do things together is inseparable from the partnership concept. This can take the form of mobilising support for an individual or action on behalf of a group. That part of a social network which is mobilised for specific purposes like this can be described as an action set. 'An action set may be looked upon as an aspect of the personal [or group/ organisational] network isolated in terms of a specific short-term instrumentally defined interactional content' (Mitchell, 1969, p.40).

Mobilising 'responses to adversity' (Barclay, 1982, p.xiii) or transforming social networks into action sets, cannot always be left to that nebulous creature 'the community'. Ways often need to be found of helping those involved to work actively together. This is what is sometimes referred to as 'interweaving' (Bayley, 1978, p.31). Action sets of all kinds frequently need to be coordinated, whether they are composed of professionals, volunteers or service users. Coordination is the key to case management, but it is also a vital ingredient of community action, the formation of self-advocacy networks or cooperation between agencies in order to meet the needs of 'children in need'. As such, it usually has to be a part of any action set strategy. It should not be assumed that coordination requires a single coordinator or that the individual or group asking for help or inviting the assistance/ participation of others is always the coordinator of the action set; for example, the Swedish Project showed that a very effective pattern of mobilisation can exist based purely on mutual support and an intuitive grasp of how those involved should work together.

At a meeting of the HIV network which referred to itself as 'the HIV world of Stockholm' it became clear that there was such a high level of trust and interpersonal responsiveness that it was very difficult to identify any particular coordinating roles, although there was plenty of evidence of what was referred to as *samverka* or 'cooperation'. The network members themselves identified the following as the glue which held the network together and to some extent took the place of formal coordination: 'trust', 'reciprocity', 'familiarity', including a sense of shared history, 'informal socialising' and a strong sense of individual 'professional identity'.

It may be that the difference between an action set able to coordinate itself and one requiring the services of a specific coordinator is related to the difference between one recruited from those already known to one another and one based on a newly created 'brokerage network' (Srinivas and Beteille, 1964) where the process of mobilisation involves creating links between quite distinct networks and the role of the broker is critical. Brokerage and coordination may therefore be closely associated with one another.

Liaison can sometimes appear to be remarkably marginal to the process of mobilising resources. The results of the North London Project suggested that in some situations there can be no relationship at all between the practical business of obtaining resources for clients and the more nebulous activities which were described as 'liaison' (Trevillion, 1996a, pp.99–100). In contrast, the Swedish Project identified relatively few formal liaison activities but a strong link between informal networking and the creation of a mobilisation potential. There is evidence from the Swedish Project that informal networking seems capable of generating trust even between potential partners who may never have met and the presence of trust seems to be the critical element in ensuring that requests for help emanating from one part of a network are met with a positive response from other parts of the network (Trevillion and Green, 1998, p.114).

At the inter-agency level, it has been suggested that establishing partnerships in the context of Health Action Zones may enable system redesign to take place, ensuring that the mobilisation of inter-agency resources is made more effective (Peck and Poxton, 1998, p.11). However, it will be important to ensure that health issues are 'owned' by the whole network, or we may find that, by marginalising the involvement of certain organisations, the issues associated with them also become marginalised and the work of the whole partnership becomes distorted. This has been the experience of Area Child Protection Committees (Sanders *et al.*, 1997) and the same thing could happen to Health Action Zones.

Mobilisation of network resources can mean many things. It may involve actively brokering a 'care package' or it may mean simply helping potential activists to get in touch and stay in touch with one another, so that they are in a position to work together when they need to do so. Overall, it means thinking and planning ahead and investing in the future.

The role of the networker in the network

So far this account of networking as a practice theory has focused largely on activities and processes. But to what extent is networking a distinctive practice role? A networker does not have a role in the sense that a doctor, lawyer or psychotherapist has a role. Nobody is employed as a networker and nobody, when asked to name their profession or occupation, is likely to say 'networker'. Networking is always a process which someone engages in as part of another role. Care managers can be networkers but so can community workers and nobody can be a networker if they do not have some other role compatible with networking.

But although networking is not a conventional role, it certainly has some role implications. This should already be clear from the way in which these activities have been described. A care manager who networks behaves in a very different kind of way from one who simply packages care through formal purchasing and contracting mechanisms. A community worker who networks behaves very differently from one who works only with formally constituted community organisations. Moreover, those who work with a networker tend to develop a different set of expectations about how he or she will relate to them than they would otherwise do.

Networking tends to create a new kind of social environment. If it is successful, it develops a much higher quality/quantity of cross-boundary linkage between organisations and institutions than previously existed and these new kinds of relations will tend to change the overall pattern of roles associated with these 'sets', including the role of the networker. If the networker is replaced by someone else, that person will inherit a very different set of role-based expectations as a result of the networker's activities. For all these reasons it is possible to talk about a networking role, provided the peculiarities of the role are acknowledged.

It may be easier to take on a networking role if the networker occupies a relatively powerful position in a social network, but networking itself tends to equalise power relations because it operates horizontally across and between organisational, professional and sectoral boundaries. It can therefore be defined in terms of its flattening effects on status differences and, for this reason, it may of course be resisted by those seeking to preserve the status quo. Associated with this is the important point that networking is not a management role, although it may help a network to manage complex relationships. Some of these points may become clearer in the next chapter, which discusses networking in relation to the assessment task.

3 Assessment: a networking approach

Linking the micro to the macro

Network assessment is a form of 'community assessment', but, unlike most examples of 'community assessment', it emphasises the continuity of the links between the individual and the community without either denying important differences between individuals or relegating the 'community' to the status merely of background information.

By the 1970s, 'community assessments' were commonplace in social work, community work and various branches of nursing (Reinhardt and Quinn, 1973, pp.174–5) and yet attempts to develop a community approach to the assessment task have been dogged by the problem of satisfactorily linking the micro-world of the individual and the macro-world of politics, economics and the environment. One example of this is community care, where it is now widely recognised that there needs to be a shift towards 'needs-based planning' linking together individual and collective definitions of need in an integrated way (Bibbington and Tarvey, 1996, p.3).

But the models of 'community assessment' which have been developed have tended to focus on collective as opposed to individual need. One attempt to recognise the diversity of 'communities' is the 'needs auditing' approach associated with the Institute for Public Policy Research: 'a needs audit seeks to identify and highlight these differences, to attempt to reconcile them where possible, and to negotiate a consensus about problems and priorities' (Percy-Smith and Sanderson, 1992, p.43). But no amount of discussion or even active community participation can overcome the fact that there are differences between the way in which 'needs' are manifested and experienced at different social levels, as well as connections. This should be

53

the starting point for any 'community assessment' and it is one of the strengths of the situational approach associated with networking.

The networking approach to 'community assessment' always starts with a specific situation of some kind. There is no requirement to operate with a simplistic opposition between individual and community needs or resources. Rather, the concept of 'need' is related to network patterns and the position of individuals, families or groups within these. Network assessments are always 'community assessments', not because they focus on collective as opposed to individual need, but because both needs and resources can be defined in terms of network structure. Differences of scale can be respected, but connections between needs at different levels can also be made by exploring the relationship between personal and other types of network as they nest within one another. In other words, the network concept enables the most personal of problems to be seen in community terms and the most political of questions to be seen partly in terms of interpersonal interaction.

It has been suggested that social workers and others should see society as a complex network and that this will enable them to 'cut across traditional categories such as casework and community development based as they have been on the reification of the individual and community respectively' (Lane, 1997, p.334). There is no need to abandon the concepts of 'the individual' and 'the community' altogether, but by relating these traditional concepts to social networks of varying shapes, sizes and complexity it is possible to define the assessment task in quite a new way which does indeed 'cut across the traditional categories' of 'casework and community development'.

Negotiating an assessment partnership

One feature of networking, which it shares with community profiling, is that assessment is not something which is done to others but something which is always undertaken in partnership with others. For networkers, the partnership principle is as much a feature of the process of assessment as it is of the goals of assessment. This does not mean that networkers do not formulate their own ideas about situations, but it does mean that they are always prepared to negotiate about them, and the very first thing that needs to be negotiated is the assessment partnership itself. Negotiating the assessment partnership involves gaining access to the network, defining the network and legitimating the network (getting permission to operate as a partnership) and these processes often take the form of a number of distinct activities:

- identifying and negotiating with community gatekeepers (access),
- identifying and negotiating a focus and a field (definition), and
- identifying and negotiating 'roadblocks' (legitimation).

Community gatekeepers

Under some circumstances, community gatekeepers may act as 'middlemen' or, presumably, middlewomen (Rodman and Courts, 1983). They may use their central position within their own networks to act as mediators between what could be seen as a 'sub-culture' and the world of social welfare professionals.

Professionals need community contacts and some contacts will be more useful than others. The specific question which social workers or other professionals always need to address is: who are the gatekeepers? Who are the people who have it in their power to block communication with important sections of the community but who could provide community access? Whoever they are, creating the conditions for effective assessment work will involve identifying an exchange of some kind in which the needs of the gatekeepers are met at the same time as the conditions for an assessment partnership are created. Here is one example.

Home helps who live in the area in which they also work can be seen as community gatekeepers. But they are often also useful mediators between social services departments, on the one hand, and local residents on the other. I was involved in developing home help/social worker liaison projects in two different local authorities in the 1980s. These projects attempted to provide a context in which social workers could relate to home helps as neighbourhood brokers. Social workers made themselves available when home helps came to the office and in this way developed a network of contacts with a number of key home helps.

Social workers gave advice and information about social security benefits, sheltered housing and other 'practical' issues and also offered consultation and support with more complex and stressful situations. Home helps, for their part, alerted social workers to particular issues and problems. Slowly but surely – and without having, at first, to do more than meet home helps – the social workers involved in the liaison were able to become part of the communication network linking the home helps to a large number of vulnerable people and those involved with supporting them, in one way or another.

This illustrates an important truth about networking, in general, and assessment partnerships, in particular. Long-term mutual benefits are rarely sufficient, in themselves, to create the conditions for partnership. Without losing sight of the long term, immediate attention needs to be paid to the subjective needs of those involved. Where those concerned are gatekeepers, it is absolutely critical that their needs are correctly identified.

In the above example, it seems likely that, because home helps themselves felt helped, they were able to work more effectively. The negotiation process, handled appropriately, ushers in a 'virtuous circle' in which positive responses to the needs of gatekeepers make it more and more likely that they will cooperate in ensuring a constant flow of increasingly useful information. Sometimes the gatekeeper will be a carer, sometimes another professional; sometimes there will be more than one gatekeeper. But across a whole range of situations, from inter-agency work to case management, it seems as if assessment is dependent upon an ability to negotiate with community gatekeepers/mediators.

Focus and field

For networkers, the individual is always part of a social field of some kind. This immediately seems to suggest that the focus is a social field as well, but this would be a false conclusion to draw. The only occasions when the focus is likely to be a network are when networking is undertaken within, and on behalf of, a closed group of some kind.

In a residential home for older people, the officer-in-charge might network with and on behalf of all the residents to facilitate new patterns of living involving more cooperation and collective activity. So long as the work was entirely focused on the residents as a whole and their relationships with one another, we could say that the focus was the network. One could say the same for any sub-groups set up for particular purposes, such as reminiscence groups. For the most part, this kind of activity is best described as groupwork rather than networking. However, even in this area of work, field and focus may overlap, rather than being absolutely identified with one another.

One project in which I was involved included both residents of a particular home and some older people living in the surrounding area. The aim of the project was to collectively explore memories and the project was established as a result of networking across the residential home/community boundary. It was not this, however, which created the distinction between field and focus, but rather the need to involve a number of professional and non-professional brokers in the bringing together of these older people, as a group. The field therefore included a wide range of people who were not the focus of the work, but were there to facilitate the work.

In other situations, the difference between field and focus is even more obvious. There might be a need to network on behalf of the specific interests of specific groups of residents – not against the interests of others, but rather to challenge disadvantage and discrimination within a home. For example, the isolated position of black elders within a predominantly white home might lead the officer-in-charge to network on their behalf.

Networking would be undertaken with the residents as a whole but on behalf of black residents. It might still be appropriate to see the residents, as a whole, as a partnership, because they would all need to be involved in any anti-racist initiatives, but the primary focus of concern and commitment would at this time be the black residents. If the work involved challenging racist stereotypes or confronting individual residents with the unacceptable nature of their behaviour, this distinction between client and community partnership would become very obvious.

Another circumstance which might create a distinction between focus and field would be the need to break down barriers between the home and the rest of the community. This means paying attention to the links residents had with family and friends (Douglas, 1986, p.131) and the new relationships that might be established with people living outside the home in terms of shared interests of one kind or another.

One particularly dynamic and progressive officer-in-charge of a home in South London worked closely with me on ways of implementing these kinds of ideas during the 1980s. She constantly 'scanned' the local environment for opportunities to develop links with a wide range of individuals and organisations outside the home, in order to facilitate the growth of an overlapping set of networks drawing the neighbourhood into the home and drawing the residents into the wider social space of the neighbourhood.

Differentiating between the concepts of focus and field solves one problem but creates another one. If the focus is not the field or, to be precise, is only part of the field, how do we go about identifying those others who might be considered part of the field? Identifying the focus enables us to identify the field. In Chapter 1, it was pointed out that a personal network can be analysed in terms of 'primary', 'secondary' or 'tertiary' stars. The field will normally include at least some of the first, if not the second or third of these 'stars'. But it may also include others, not yet involved, including professionals or official agencies of one kind or another. Initial discussions will soon highlight those who want, or need, to be involved in any partnership activity. In this way, the assessment partnership is recruited from the field. One way of thinking about this is that the core of the assessment partnership is likely to be an action set capable of mobilising its efforts on behalf of the focus around which it has formed.

This can be illustrated with reference to the styles of work pioneered with people living with and affected by HIV and AIDS, where the concepts of field and focus turn out to be highly compatible with the model of 'flexible, augmentative social care planning' in which all 'social legal, health and interpersonal networks' are included (Gaitley and Seed, 1989, p.14) and which is supposed to enable social workers, nurses and others to grasp the pattern or 'gestalt' of the total situation (ibid., p.15).

The following is based on an account relayed to me by the social worker. The details have been changed to protect confidentiality.

John is about to leave hospital, having partially recovered from a serious infection. He is able to move around with some difficulty, but is breathless and easily tired. He wants to return home to his flat on a council estate where he lives alone. A former lover and some friends might be prepared to offer limited support but there is little likelihood of family support as there has been no contact between him and his family since they discovered he was gay ten years before. Although some attempt could be made to reinvolve the family, it seems likely that much of the care needed will have to come from statutory and voluntary organisations. John is closely involved in the process of defining who should be involved as partners in the assessment process but, on the whole, accepts the advice he receives from the social worker.

In this case the assessment is undertaken in partnership with those who are likely to play a part in the 'care package' which John will need. Volunteers, a district nurse, the general practitioner, a home help organiser, an occupational therapist and a housing officer could all be worked with as an assessment partnership and much may depend on an effective inter-agency network to which managers will need to contribute. Links between health and social services are likely to be particularly important.

The concept of the assessment field is open enough to include a number of individuals, groups or agencies who may be prepared to participate as informants, but who may not want or need to be involved at a later stage. We therefore need to keep in mind a distinction between the eventual action set, mobilised to meet the needs of an individual or group, and the broader field. Nevertheless, involving people as partners at the assessment stage may make it much more likely that they will stay involved.

Awareness of many of these issues appears to be quite widespread, particularly within the area of HIV work. Whereas the previous example was based on material from London, the Swedish *kurators* pointed out that 'we also have a strategy ... to involve persons around the patient, the network, even if, maybe, it's a theoretical network'.

These examples illustrate what can happen when there is little or no conflict between social worker and service user about the choice of partners, but what if there were such a conflict and it was not possible to resolve it? The answer has to be that, if service users do not give permission for other people to be approached with a view to contributing to the assessment process, then, in the absence of any issues which might override it – child abuse, evidence of mental illness and so on – this has to be respected. This may be particularly relevant in relation to work with people living with HIV and AIDS.

Identifying and negotiating roadblocks

When someone outside the context of the existing assessment partnership intervenes to block its work, the assessment process is brought to a halt as if the road ahead were blocked. When this happens, we need to follow the trail of resistance back to its source and reorient the framework of assessment so that it takes account of this resistance.

An attempt by social workers to liaise with district nurses or health visitors to explore joint staffing of 'family advice sessions' at a local community centre may initially meet with an enthusiastic response, but, as some of the implications begin to emerge, the health workers may become much less enthusiastic. Communication becomes increasingly awkward and meetings less and less productive. It turns out that a number of senior managers are not happy about the project and are effectively blocking it. The nurses and health visitors will therefore not be able to participate in the assessment exercise unless they get 'permission' from their seniors to do so.

Communication will continue to be muffled unless the social workers and their managers succeed in negotiating 'permission' for discussions to continue with the relevant health service managers. This 'permission' might only be granted if they themselves are involved in some of the meetings and then it might be possible to openly discuss any concerns they might have without these acting as a general block on all communication. An assessment partnership must be inclusive of all those who might have an interest in its work and the power either to advance or to block it.

Sometimes assessment may become blocked simply because some people feel they cannot express their true feelings or their real needs. To deal with situations like this, a social worker will need to attend to implicit, as well as explicit, messages.

Many carers may feel that they have little choice but to care for aged and infirm parents, spouses and children. When asked directly, they might well say that they want to continue caring for their dependent relative. But anyone seeking to put together an appropriate 'care package' in such a situation who simply took this at face value and did not pay attention to 'process' clues such as tiredness, frustration, anger or depression would be likely to miss an important part of the message, that part which says, 'I feel exhausted, trapped, devalued and unhelped by everyone, including you!' Messages like this are silenced because they are in conflict with assumptions about the way carers ought to feel in our 'patriarchal' society (Gittins, 1985, p.131) and this has been reflected in the way professionals have ignored the needs of carers (Hicks, 1988).

How does an assessment partnership work?

It is impossible to lay down hard-and-fast rules about situations as varied as those described in this book, but the networking approach to assessment can be characterised in two ways:

- as a process of integrating diverse perspectives to produce one multi-dimensional picture which can form the basis of any collective action undertaken by the partnership;
- as a process of continual feedback which constantly deconstructs and reconstructs the network picture, either by filling in the assessment 'gaps' or by transforming the network picture entirely.

The feedback process raises individual and collective awareness and one consequence is that the networking approach to assessment is educational.

When people begin to build up a picture of how things are now, and how they might be different in the future, they are educating and empowering themselves. But surely, different viewpoints imply conflict? Can there be an assessment partnership if some of the partners are in conflict with one another? The answer is 'yes', and the assessment might be all the better as a result.

As a social worker in West London in the 1980s, I once had a client, an elderly woman living alone, who was gradually withdrawing from responsibility for her own life. I felt, rightly or wrongly, that those involved with her had to do everything possible to reverse this process. Another social worker involved in the assessment partnership disagreed with me vehemently, feeling, rightly or wrongly, that decline was irreversible and that we should collectively assume responsibility for the client's welfare. As a result, the way in which 'facts' were interpreted was open to constant challenge.

Because neither of us was in a position to impose our views on others involved in the situation, and because we were both committed to the partnership, we were both exposed to pressure from other members of the partnership to compromise and to explore the middle ground. The partnership not only survived the conflict, but ensured that the assessment and planning process was undertaken from a much more realistic perspective than would have been possible if either I or the other social worker had had sole responsibility for the assessment.

Gathering and analysing information

Having established the conditions for assessment through negotiation, it is time to move on to the next stage, which involves the assessment process itself. What kind of information do we need? Network assessments require both 'hard', or relatively objective, information and 'soft', relatively subjective, information.

'Hard' information covers anything which might help us to understand how the characteristics of a particular network mesh together with the likely effects of particular interventions upon it. We are therefore likely to be interested in such things as the pattern of interaction, the frequency of interaction, the role of brokers in linking together different parts of the network mesh, the way information flows around the system and whether or not 'action sets' exist. But as we are interested in facilitating community partnership, we are also likely to be interested in working out how specific interventions on our part might help to promote patterns of partnership in all these areas.

'Soft' information is just as important as 'hard' information. When the assessment task involves 'joining' an existing social network, we may think of the networker as a 'controlled participant observer' (Moreno, 1978, p.109) experiencing all the currents of thought and feeling flowing through that network. This kind of 'soft' or process knowledge is an example of the reflexivity associated with networking and often plays a significant role in assessing what needs to be done to create an assessment partnership. It is likely that many views and experiences effectively silenced by feelings of powerlessness will only be discovered through reflecting on 'process'

The five-dimensional model of community assessment incorporates the following:

- interpersonal and interactional data,
- community data,
- information about the flexibility and responsiveness of systems,
- information about communication patterns, and
- data on mobilisation potential.

Gathering and making sense of interpersonal and interactional data

Social fields of various kinds contain large amounts of information and, by analysing the way in which individuals link with one another, we can begin to understand the forms of interdependency which characterise a particular social field. How should we go about gathering this kind of data? A number of techniques are available, some designed for in-depth work, others to produce rapid results.

Network diaries

These come in many different shapes and sizes, but should enable individuals to keep track of who they interact with, how, why, what their various relationships mean to them and, ideally, provide some space to enable those involved to consider alternative or additional contacts (Beresford and Trevillion, 1995, pp.39–52). Whatever form the diary takes, it is vital that the diary-keeping process includes some opportunity for those keeping these records to discuss and reflect on what they are producing. Diaries can provide excellent raw material for further groupwork sessions (ibid., pp.53–66).

The main benefit of the diary approach is that it provides very detailed and specific data, together with opportunities for reflective discussion about relationship needs and opportunities. One weakness, however, is that, unless all key members of a network are simultaneously keeping diaries, the picture of interpersonal relationships which will be built up will inevitably correspond to the subjective perceptions of the diary keeper. This may be acceptable if that is our main interest, but it may lead to important information about other issues, such as constraints on caring or parenting, being missed out or only loosely described. The main drawback of the method, however, is that in my experience it takes a minimum of three or four weeks to generate meaningful data. Where there is a pressing need for intervention, a network diary is unlikely to be the most appropriate assessment tool.

Network questionnaires

This method of network assessment involves making use of a standardised checklist of questions designed to reveal information about the quantity and quality of interpersonal links. All the data which can be obtained through a diary in an indirect way can, at least in principle, be obtained through a questionnaire directly and in a fraction of the time required for diary keeping.

Questionnaires can generate a mass of data (Trevillion, 1996a). Unfortunately, like diaries, questionnaires have to be administered simultaneously to several members of a network in order to overcome the problems of selectivity of data outlined above. A more fundamental problem is that use of a questionnaire can appear disrespectful and, even in a research context, does not provide many opportunities for individuals to reflect on the significance of their relationships. The lack of time for thought and reflection can also shift the balance of power rather too far towards the interviewer and away from the interviewee.

All these problems can be overcome in a research or development project, but may be more intractable in practice. In addition, the very lack of time which militates against diary keeping might be thought to make for an atmosphere which is decidedly unconducive to an emotionally neutral survey of network relationships. If there is an element of urgency, there may also be so much pressure for intervention at a practical or emotional level that it is difficult to see how satisfactory answers can be obtained.

Network tracking

Network tracking does not require any materials other than a blank sheet of paper and can be incorporated in a standard professional interview. It simply involves following up all relationship data with some characteristic questions. (How often do you see X? When did you last see X? Who is X closest to?) It is often appropriate and helpful to build in reflexive questions. (How do you feel about your relationship with X? How would you change your relationship with X?) If possible, those using this method should try to explore unmet needs both in terms of existing relationships and in terms of imagined relationships.

Excursions into fantasy, often prefaced by a comment such as 'How would you like your relationships to be different? can generate sometimes startling insights into the gap between the way relationships are ordered and how individuals would like their needs to be met. Even if time is pressing, helpful data on social fields can be generated in this way, often by single interviews. If there are opportunities to meet and work with individuals named by the client or other initial respondent, even richer and more multifaceted assessments can be produced.

Gathering and making sense of community data

In the previous chapter, the community dimension of networking was discussed in terms of the overlapping categories of identity, power and social support. These form the basis of this aspect of the assessment process.

Identity

Where individuals or groups feel alone with their problems, even though they may have access to material resources, it may well reflect problems with the social field. As the kind of information we are interested in relates to specific social fields rather than philosophy or politics, it will normally be more effective to find ways of asking questions about identity in the context of specific relationships or patterns of social interaction, such as 'Do you find that you identify with X and Y?' or 'Do you feel you have something in common with X or Y?'

The information yielded by diaries, questionnaires or other techniques for recording interaction patterns can be used to generate these kinds of questions in follow-up interviews.

Of course, there are many issues of identity which have less to do with patterns of social interaction than with personal memories or strongly felt political or religious beliefs. These 'psychological networks' or 'imagined communities' (Anderson, 1983) should always be taken account of in any assessment, but constitute a subject of their own which is only loosely connected with networking. The contrast between the 'psychological' and 'interactive' network may, however, be very revealing and informative.

Power

From a networking perspective, it is important that empowerment is seen not as a zero sum game in which power is transferred from one person to another. This traditional way of thinking is based too literally on Weber's discovery that power is relational. Rather, we need to see empowerment in more creative terms as a qualitative shift in the relationship between individuals and the social environment such that they feel they can 'make a difference'. From this point of view, any assessment of power in social fields should take the form of exploring what kind of opportunities exist for positive feedback loops which would enable individuals engaged in forms of social action to experience themselves as being able to 'make a difference'. The aim would not be simply to measure degrees of empowerment, but also to explore the potential for creating new pathways linking disempowered individuals and groups to sources of social power.

As with identity, abstract questioning about power is unlikely to deliver interesting answers. Usually, it will be more appropriate to explore the subjective meaning given to specific action sequences and to evaluate them with other members of the assessment partnership in terms of 'making a difference'. One way of doing this is through the use of *hypotheticals*. A hypothetical is simply an imaginary situation. In this case, a hypothetical could be used to explore by a process of question and answer whether a new pattern of linkages would 'make a difference' and open up new opportunities to the disempowered individual or group.

Mutual support

It is unwise to assume that close-knit patterns of social interaction always generate social support. But, on the other hand, loose-knit social fields are far less likely to be associated with social support than close-knit ones. Therefore, in any effort to try and gauge the degree of mutual support in a social field, it is normally helpful to have some overall measure of 'connectedness'. This can be done by making use of the interaction data already gathered through diaries, questionnaires or 'network tracking'. Having established this, it is then necessary to explore in more depth the degree to which key individuals actually experience their relationships as supportive and the degree to which they conceive of support not simply in terms of specific individuals but in terms of collective processes. This kind of data is only likely to emerge in the context of a process of reflection upon 'connectedness' which it is not always easy to justify or explain when time is short and needs are pressing. Therefore it will normally be more effective to link this process to particular events. Individuals can be asked whom they find most supportive and in what ways that support is actually made tangible. They can also be asked if there had been any occasions when they were able to reciprocate that support.

If the answers to these questions seem to reveal an absence of supportive community relationships, the assessment should focus on ways of generating increased levels of support. In this connection, use could also be made of hypotheticals and, if so, it will probably be practical to integrate work on support with work on empowerment. In any case, the connections between the different aspects of community are such that it would be unwise to regard them as mutually exclusive categories.

Flexibility and responsiveness

Discovering the extent to which a social field incorporates flexibility, informality and responsiveness may start with accounts of personal experiences, but should also extend into a form of critical path analysis which involves wide ranging discussions.

Critical path analysis for networkers

At root, this approach is concerned with tracking an issue or problem across the organisational landscape, taking particular note of what happens at the boundary between different organisations. But, whereas conventional critical path analysis focuses solely on what happens to the issue or problem, the real aim of this assessment exercise is to discover information about structures and systems. In order to do this effectively, the assessment partnership should ideally include members of the various organisations involved, especially if the behaviour of these organisations is deemed to be of continuing interest. Positive indicators might include speed of organisational response, openness of the organisation to lateral or peer contact and communication, willingness to engage in informal as well as formal discussions and communications, and so on.

As always, with networking the aim is to move rapidly from assessment to intervention, and any problems identified should lead on to the development of particular networking strategies designed to overcome them.

Information about communication patterns

Communication is almost as varied as life itself, but to point this out is not particularly helpful unless some attempt is made to provide tools which can render this complexity intelligible. On the other hand, the subject of communication seems also to lend itself to a kind of lazy overgeneralisation. It is almost too easy to blame 'communication problems' for any failures in the social welfare system and doing so seems to make it harder to identify the real issues.

The social network approach tries to overcome these difficulties by focusing on some key characteristics of the communication network and using this as a way of gaining information about communication patterns and processes. In Chapter 2, it was argued that it was important to know whether a communication circuit was 'closed' or 'open' and where the barriers to communication flows actually lay. Building on this, it is possible to see that information about communication networks can be obtained from the following:

- exploring the overall shape or pattern of communication, noting the relationship between this and specific patterns of access to and exclusion from information;
- exploring the specific characteristics of specific (dyadic) communication linkages;
- exploring the relationship between overall communication patterns and communication content; and
- exploring the relationship between the characteristics of a particular linkage and communication content.

All the data on interaction collected through diaries, questionnaires or network tracking can provide information on communication networks. However, obtaining a holistic picture may be very difficult unless some attempt is made to obtain information from a variety of sources.

In general, networkers should try to encourage an experimental approach to communication issues among members of the assessment partnership as they seek to move from the assessment stage into the planning process. Use could be made of a hypothetical to explore whether or not it would be helpful to reorganise the way all involved communicated with one another. If it could be shown that new patterns or styles of communication created new opportunities for individual service users, this process of 'experimentation' could be quite a powerful mechanism for promoting change, especially if the whole process were conducted in a network conference or some other face-to-face setting.

Gathering information on mobilisation potential

Networking is a very practical activity. We are interested not only in who knows who, but also in the extent to which individuals and groups can call upon others for assistance. Moreover, the assessment process focuses not only on what is but also on what could be. An individual may currently be unable to call on many people for help, but under some circumstances this might change. Networkers pose the question: under what circumstances or conditions might an existing social network be transformed into an action set? Analysing mobilisation patterns and mobilisation potential is an important part of the assessment process.

Sometimes all that is required is to observe closely what is already happening. If a mobilisation process is under way, all that is needed is to ensure that you understand how it works and who is involved. This may not always be straightforward, but attention to the issues already outlined in this book should be sufficient to enable patterns and processes to be charted. However, in many cases, the fact that help has been sought from a professional indicates that mobilisation processes have been relatively ineffective. In such a situation, the networker needs to understand mobilisation issues while very little mobilisation appears to be going on. In such a situation, use can be made of hypotheticals which focus on specified changes in the social network.

For example, an isolated former psychiatric patient may be very lonely and may tell his or her social worker that his response to his feelings of rejection by the wider community will be to stay home alone, drinking and watching television. However, if a hypothetical change in his situation were introduced to him, such as closer coordination between the mental health services and his family or ways in which former inmates of the same psychiatric hospital could contact one another, he might then be encouraged to explore his reactions to this changed situation and new mobilisation strategies might emerge as a result.

Avoiding mechanistic approaches

For the sake of convenience, the various aspects of assessment have been presented separately, but it would be quite wrong to give the reader the impression that these activities can be carried on in isolation from one another. The networking approach to assessment is an integrated one, through which knowledge and understanding of one issue is connected with another. Nor would I like anyone reading this chapter to believe that networking consists simply of using one or other of the assessment tools I have briefly described. With the possible exception of network diaries, none of them is available in a complete form, for use 'off the peg'. My hope is that practitioners may use the descriptions I have given of ways of assessing networks as a spur to their own creativity, rather than as a model to be rigidly or mechanistically copied.

4 Community brokers

Brokering task communities

Networkers can be found in a wide range of settings, taking part in a wide range of activities, but whatever the context of their work they will frequently be found acting as brokers: brokers of people, brokers of information and brokers of resources. Inasmuch as all forms of networking are concerned with forging links across boundaries, it could be argued that all forms of networking are a kind of brokerage. However, this ignores the strategic role played by brokers. Those networks which can be defined as 'complex' or 'brokerage networks' come into being and depend for their continued existence on specific brokers (Eisenstadt and Roniger, 1980, p.43). While many people can actively participate in cross-boundary work to the benefit of a particular network, brokers are significant in situations where the network relies upon the strategic linking work of a particular individual, organisation or group.

We are concerned here only with forms of brokerage which are relevant to the field of social welfare. So as to distinguish this type of brokerage from that which is concerned with political manipulation and ways of 'circumventing formal structures' (Komito, 1992, p.140) the term 'community brokerage' will be used to describe the strategic linking work which is associated with the development of community partnerships and the building of 'task communities'.

This type of linking work has been compared to the way a spider builds a web. The West London Project asked a number of different interprofessional groups to contribute to a general definition of strategic linking work. One of the most striking comments made was that it was like building 'a web'.

71

This was later elaborated on and became 'creating a web with a common thread so that all the parts are linked together as a whole, dependent on one another' (Beresford and Trevillion, 1995, p.64).

While this is a memorable image and it conveys the notion of interdependency very well, it tends to imply that the community broker is rather like a spider spinning his or her web. Apart from its slightly sinister overtones, this image exaggerates the power of the community broker. A spider creates its own web but a community broker simply connects existing organisations/networks/services with one another. He or she may supply some strategic threads, but the raw materials of the web are there already. The best examples of community brokerage may lead to the development of some dazzlingly complex networks, but the expertise of the community broker lies in the process of making connections.

Community brokerage is perhaps therefore more appropriately defined as the process of making and maintaining the strategic links on which complex networks of separate individuals, groups or organisations depend for their continued existence. The role of the community broker has a number of components, each of which can be seen as a role or role set: brokering change, promoting network education, encouraging power sharing and facilitating network reflexivity.

Brokering change

Brokering change involves making change by forging new kinds of links. All the most significant features of brokering change can be present when working with those who are already involved in a situation, but not in any form of contact or communication with one another, as in the following case study dating from the 1980s.

Henrietta Plowden was a woman of 84 who lived alone in sheltered accommodation. She had Alzheimer's Disease and would not allow anyone except her daughter-in-law to shop, clean or cook for her. Although the situation had remained relatively stable for some time, it was at considerable cost to the emotional and physical well-being of her daughter-in-law. However, some months after assuming responsibility for coordinating the few services which played any part in supporting this elderly woman, I became aware that a 'crisis' was looming in the shape of the very reasonable desire of the daughter-in-law to go away on holiday for two weeks with her immediate family and so I called a 'network conference'.

Although conscious of the possible risks to Henrietta Plowden, my feeling was that this 'crisis' might be an opportunity to establish a more equitable and effective partnership. I therefore approached the conference with the intention of exploring whether it might not be possible to involve the home help, a volunteer visitor and the warden of the sheltered housing scheme much more closely than in the past.

The idea was to use the conference as a vehicle for bringing together the various parties in a way which would enable the pattern of support to be renegotiated and enable the daughter-in-law to feel that she was not responsible for everything to do with her welfare. The aim was to solve both the immediate 'crisis' precipitated by the daughter-in-law's holiday and the longer-term problems relating to the overconcentration of care in one part of the network, by facilitating the development of a more 'interwoven' network.

But having a strategy and seizing an opportunity are not enough. There also needs to be a clear plan of action. This is never easy to develop when all involved are very worried and when there is no previous history of successful partnership and collaboration. In this case, there were the added problems of enabling the daughter-in-law to feel she could trust the professionals to take more responsibility and persuading her to accept help from 'strangers'. Eventually, the following plan was designed.

The daughter-in-law was to be accompanied by the home help – whom the client normally only allowed to make a cup of tea – on several visits to her mother-in-law prior to going on holiday. By sharing tasks with the daughter-in-law on these visits, the home help might be accepted as a substitute by the client in the daughter-in-law's absence. On her return, the daughter-in-law was not to resume all her previous tasks but, rather, only some of them. If successful, a similar procedure was to be used to introduce other underused helpers and to enable them to play a fuller part in supporting Henrietta Plowden.

Looking back on this process now, it seems as if I was taking on the role of brokering change by establishing new strategic links between those who had previously had little to do with one another. Inasmuch as those links could not have been developed by anyone else at that point, the resulting complex network could be seen as continuing to depend to a considerable extent on the way in which those links were constantly nurtured by my own brokering activities, either within the conference or outside it. The case therefore fits well with the model outlined at the beginning of the chapter.

Looked at in more detail, it is possible to see that the brokering of net-work change involved two distinct sub-roles, problem solving and change legitimation. The first was associated with network analysis and change management, whereas the second was associated with the process of achieving a mandate for change from the stakeholders

Problem solving/network analysis

Network problem solving involves engaging the network in the process of assessing both problems and solutions and putting problem-solving ideas into practice through the development of new patterns of linkage. As well as channelling new resources into a situation, this may take the form of reorganising the pattern of existing resources. In this case, time was spent ensuring that everybody had a good grasp of the pattern of daily and weekly interaction, including the number and type of tasks for which individuals were responsible, how often certain tasks had to performed and the qualitative features of particular interactions such as the intensity of emotion associated with them (likely to be in inverse proportion to the ease with which they could be transferred to somebody else).

Problem solving/managing change

However strong the case for change, the experience of it, which always involves loss, can be overwhelming (Toffler, 1971, pp.28–51) and resistance to change is often born out of this fear of drowning in it and losing control. Here it was possible to work towards change while anticipating resistance to it both from Henrietta Plowden and, perhaps less obviously, from other members of the caring network, including the daughter-in-law.

Although Henrietta Plowden, her daughter-in-law and the home help were all asked to make changes in the way they related to one another, nobody was asked to make so many changes that they were likely to feel they had lost control of the pace of change. The sharing of tasks rather than simply insisting that one person hand over responsibility to another also seems to have made a major contribution to the change management process.

Legitimating change: achieving a mandate for change from the stakeholders

In any situation, change will be resisted if it is seen as counter to the interests or wishes of those who are most closely involved. All those with a stake in a situation should ideally be brought into the process of discussing possible changes before they are implemented, so as to ensure that well intentioned interventions are not immediately undermined or rejected by key stakeholders. Just because change is on a small scale and involves individuals rather than organisations, this does not mean that there are no 'stakeholders'.

Here all the key players, including Henrietta Plowden, had a 'stake' in the outcome. For the daughter-in-law, her role as carer was at issue and she was concerned to protect her role while also reducing the scale of her responsibilities. For the home help and the home care organiser, what was at stake was justifying their use of time on this particular client and whether they were using their skills and resources in an appropriate way. For Henrietta Plowden, what was at issue was all her fears about herself and her future, while for me, as the social worker, what was at stake was achieving a viable care plan in line with the needs and expectations of everyone involved, while also respecting the needs, wishes and sensitivities of the client.

The process of achieving a mandate had to be an inclusive one and, in this case, the choice of a network conference seems to have facilitated this. While it may not be necessary always to hold such a conference, in this situation it is difficult to see how the process of achieving a mandate from all those involved could otherwise have occurred. The term 'mandate' should not be taken to imply that a formal declaration is necessary in every situation. However, what is needed is for the broker to achieve an explicit consensus, not only about the wisdom of specific plans, but also about the whole direction of the change process. This involves some discussion of underlying values and philosophy as well as practical details. More than anything else, as this case demonstrates, it is the process of achieving a mandate which secures a network partnership and the network conference therefore seems to have played a pivotal role both in achieving a mandate for change and in securing a supportive partnership.

Sometimes the process of legitimating change can go badly wrong, undermining the whole brokerage strategy, as in the following example, drawn from the period when I was working as a senior social worker in the 1980s.

A child protection conference was called following a perceived deterioration in the quality of care being given to a child. The conference decided on a plan which entailed a major change of role for the family aide who had been involved for some time in an informal and 'supportive' manner. This family aide was asked to explain to the parents that she would be focusing much more on surveillance and much less on general befriending than in the past. This might have been justified and probably was, but unfortunately, the family aide, who also worked for the home care service as a home help, did not realise that she might be expected to undertake this kind of work. As a result, she did not do as she was asked and when it became clear that no obvious change of role had occurred, it emerged that she had never felt happy with a decision which had been taken at a meeting in which she felt she had no power to either express her views or to believe that notice would be taken of them.

This kind of passive subversion of decisions to which everyone has apparently 'agreed' but which some network partners feel they nevertheless cannot support in practice, is in fact quite common and represents a failure of the mandating process, which leads inexorably to a breakdown, not only of particular plans, but also, frequently, of the network itself. In my experience, while powerful dissenting voices make their views known quite clearly and explicitly, the least powerful members of a network partnership may not say anything, but rather act out their unhappiness through a process of quiet subversion.

In situations like this, individuals or groups may have their own very strong views about the nature of their 'contract' with the rest of the network. An effort needs to be made to involve relatively powerless but distinctly unhappy members of a network partnership in a process of careful renegotiation, rather than ignoring them just because they have not actively opposed the plans supported by the more dominant members of the partnership.

Network education

Community brokerage can be seen as an educational role. During the initial stages of the development of a complex network, this educational role tends to take the form of developing network awareness. During the later stages it may take the form of developing action learning sets.

Developing network awareness

The process of linking individuals, groups or organisations with one another requires that some attention be given to shared awareness. When this does not take place, attempts to pursue joint action tend to founder.

It may seem that all those agencies involved in child sexual abuse work in a particular area would benefit from the formation of a multidisciplinary 'team' and a new network might be created consisting of police, paediatricians, psychologists and social workers. However, it may quickly emerge that all the members of this 'team' were approaching their work with different perceptions, priorities and different values. Such a network plainly needs to develop some shared understandings before it can do any useful work. This may require translation or interpreting skills.

Network interpretation

Those who speak different languages sometimes need an interpreter in order to communicate, but it is not just differences of language which sometimes lead to mutual incomprehension. Whenever we attempt to reach out to others who may not see the world in the way that we do, we may fail to communicate even though we might appear to be using the same language. It is always much easier to stereotype or caricature other people than it is make the effort to understand practices which may, at first, appear strange or mystifying. But unless someone takes the risk of trying to comprehend and then to help others to understand, it will not be possible for a community partnership to be built and this is as true of inter-agency relationships as it is of other relationships.

There are two stages involved in the process of inter-agency interpreting. The first stage is the 'ethnographic stage', in which the community broker meets and talks to the different network participants. In the case of inter-agency brokerage, this is ideally linked to a phase of 'participant observation' or unstructured time spent in the different organisational cultures. The aim is to develop one's own awareness of different perceptions, values and priorities. The second stage is the 'lingua franca stage' in which the broker actively helps the agencies to understand one another.

The relations between local authority social work teams and small voluntary organisations are often difficult because contacts are too superficial to promote a real understanding of each other's work. The model proposed here might help to overcome this kind of impasse. It might reveal to a statutory social work team that the lack of clear policy or line management accountability complained of by them in relation to a small voluntary organisation might give that organisation a flexibility and willingness to experiment which could be invaluable in setting up imaginative 'packages of care'. Simultaneously, the small voluntary organisation might discover that the 'bureaucracy' of the statutory social work team is associated with a capacity to deliver reliable and predictable services on a long-term basis that they are unable to match.

Developing action learning sets

Although it is likely that the community broker will continue to be needed for the lifetime of any complex social welfare network, it may be possible to develop the broker's educational role from that of spreading general knowledge and awareness into more focused activity in which the responsibility for learning shifts from the broker to members of the network themselves. Certain kinds of social networks can provide opportunities for mutual learning and therefore community partnerships can be seen as what have been described in other contexts as 'action learning sets' or informal peer-based learning networks (Gay, 1983).

The role of the community broker is to help organise these 'action learning sets' and to support the learning process which, if successful, is likely to enable network members to find new ways of thinking about their collective endeavours.

Power sharing

Brokerage can lead to an accumulation of power in the hands of the 'broker'. In some situations it may even be 'a step on the road to political power' (Kettering, 1986, p.55). But in a social work context, any unnecessary accumulation of power by professionals is counterproductive and certainly unlikely to facilitate the empowerment of clients who may have a 'history of powerlessness and enforced passivity' (Rose and Black, 1985, p.82). An essential community brokerage skill is therefore the ability to counteract this tendency by using one's own position as an intermediary to open up channels of communication for others, rather than to continue to monopolise communication.

Inter-agency liaisons which are conducted on a one-to-one basis have a potential to exclude other members of the organisations involved from participation. Combining regular one-to-one communication with occasional larger-scale meetings between a range of agency representatives can be helpful in preventing 'broker' monopolisation of the liaisons developing.

At the inter-agency level, the broker agency should see its liaisons as an opportunity to introduce other agencies to one another, rather than seeking to channel all inter-agency communication through itself. Fundamentally, there is a need to develop the attitude that brokerage is about opening up contact and communication.

When trying to build networks of support around individual service users, the issue of power is even more central. For example, care managers may inadvertently oppress both service users and carers if they monopolise channels of communication and fail to enable people to build their own patterns of 'connectedness' with one another.

Although it was argued at the beginning of this chapter that community brokerage is associated with complex networks which are dependent on the efforts of the broker for their continued existence, the role can be discharged in an empowering way if the emphasis moves away from control and into ways of helping people to obtain the resources they need. There is some support for this rather paradoxical role from the general sociological/social anthropological literature on brokers which emphasises that those who use brokers can be very proactive and to some extent can be seen as in control of the brokerage situation (Komito, 1992).

Facilitating network reflexivity

Brokers need to stay involved with the networks they have helped to set up, if only to monitor the continued viability of the linkages which bind it together as a 'task community'. All complex networks have a tendency towards entropy and fragmentation. It is important that networkers operating in situations like this 'take the temperature' of the network on a regular basis. The only reliable way of doing so is to ensure that the pattern of linkages includes a number of feedback loops between the broker and the brokerage network. These can be either formal or informal, but they must be robust enough to ensure that the broker receives reliable information. For their part, brokers need to be willing to recognise that there are problems and this is not always easy, particularly as, in some cases, the broker may have put a lot of time and energy into arranging for the birth of a new network and may not want to recognise that his or her 'baby' is in trouble. This process of 'taking the temperature' of the network lies at the root of network reflexivity because community brokers cannot help to spread awareness if they, themselves, are out of touch with what is going on because they do not want to face up to the truth.

Linking action sets

So far, we have concerned ourselves only with those aspects of community brokerage which relate to the creation, or continued growth, of specific complex networks. But the concept of community brokerage is much broader than this and extends to the development and management of links between 'action sets' or even between more broadly based inter-agency networks.

One of the curious features of the development of links between action sets is that they may often be haphazard or even entirely accidental by-products of other types of networking. Whereas all the other types of networks we have looked at have been purposeful, there comes a point when network dynamics can take over. In order to understand the reasons for this, we need to go back to social network theory. Social networks tend to consist of links which are multiplex rather than single stranded (Mitchell, 1969, p.4). This is almost inevitable where the number of possible links is finite. What this means for community brokerage in particular is that, as more and more community partnerships are created, they tend increasingly to overlap with one another. This has two major consequences. One is that certain key individuals become ever more closely linked with one another, and the other is that action sets, many of which will be brokerage networks, will themselves become increasingly enmeshed with one another.

This process is almost unavoidable and may have many benefits, but it would be wise to remember that one unfortunate result may be that individuals start to feel that they have lost control to rather nebulous external forces. However, one way in which individuals and organisations can empower themselves is to seek to take advantage of this process by consciously setting out to develop a series of networks, linked by brokerage, within which community partnerships may support one another. At its simplest, this type of brokerage involves single chains developed in a linear fashion, supporting a number of interrelated initiatives and overlapping networks.

Brokering single network chains

The following hypothetical case study is based on my own experiences as a social worker in West London.

A local health visitor and a locality-based social worker work with each other on complex child care cases concerning a number of homeless families temporarily living within the neighbourhood. Although they find that they often approach their work in a different way, they value each other's contributions and begin to explore the possibility of an inter-agency liaison to promote collaborative work. When they discuss this idea with their managers, they get a positive response, but it seems also that, as the major shared concern would be homeless families, the liaison should cover all those health visitors and social workers who work with this client group, many of whom live outside the boundaries of the original 'patch'.

Eventually, a number of local liaisons are started but all those involved also meet as a special interest group on a regular basis. Members of this special interest group then begin to work together on projects, one of which is the development of new crèche/playgroup facilities in some of the hotels and hostels being used to house homeless families. This project meets with an enthusiastic response from some homeless families who involve themselves in it and, over time, a number of other activities are generated.

The process of building a chain of linked networks of this kind can be seen as a process of discovery, in which the links between issues are revealed and personal and political strategies are combined. A whole range of feedback possibilities then arise, through which the issues dealt with by one partnership can inform the work done by another. In this example, the health visitor and social worker may well encourage individual clients to participate in the play space campaign or in general campaigns about homelessness, while at the same time cooperating closely in their more individualised supportive work.

Network chains like this develop incrementally over time, but in ways which allow those involved to stay in control of the overall process through their brokerage activities.

Brokering multiple network chains

Like single chains, multiple chains consist of a number of different networks and activities held together by brokerage. Unlike them, however, multiple chains do not focus on a single issue or even set of issues, but rather characteristically involve forging links between partners who may be of value to one another across a wide range of issues. Some of the best examples of this come from the heyday of patch or neighbourhood social work. I was once a member of a team in the 1980s which held regular 'patch lunches' to which many local groups and agencies were invited. The explicit purpose of these 'lunches' was to encourage more links to be made and the team in this way saw itself as brokering a neighbourhood-wide set of partnerships.

Brokering the inter-agency partnership system

Many contemporary welfare activities depend on the existence of well organised and clearly articulated partnership systems. But if such systems are to work, it is vital that all those involved have some awareness of their relationship to them. This means that the partnership system as a whole needs to be brokered. Brokering the partnership system is essentially a matter of ensuring that the parts facilitate the whole and the whole facilitates the parts. Unlike the progressive and incremental processes associated with developing network chains, this requires a more planned approach in which all aspects of the system are brokered simultaneously.

Ensuring that the partnership system works is becoming increasingly important as social policy puts an increasing emphasis on communication, cooperation and collaboration between professionals, service users, families and others. It is this emphasis which is revolutionising services for both adults and children. As far as the latter are concerned, it is clear that services to 'children in need' and their families will entail effective inter-agency collaboration, for example between housing and social services departments and between different local authorities. The issues are even clearer in relation to services for adults.

Community care: a case for systems brokerage

The care management system which is the centrepiece of the government's community care policy cannot exist in isolation. The care management partnership needs to be supported by a complex partnership system. To some extent, the need for 'a fully integrated system which is geared to the support of the care management process' is already recognised (DOH/SSI, 1991a, p.66). But, whilst it has been acknowledged that community care is not yet a 'seamless service' (DOH/SSI, 1991b, p.21), it has not yet been fully appreciated that the process of integrating 'information systems', 'service planning', 'service contracting', 'quality assurance', 'service monitoring', 'management support' and 'training' (DOH/SSI, 1991a, p.66) cannot be separated from general issues of coordination and collaboration. In other words, we need to see the community care system, as a whole, as a partnership system.

Those involved in planning accessible information services will need to be involved in discussions with libraries, advice centres, health centres and other community facilities, but they will also need to have links with social workers and others involved with service users, carers and their representatives and self-advocacy groups. They will also need to feed back to all those involved with service delivery as to whether the information which is provided is adequate or, indeed, whether it seriously misrepresents the reality of what is on offer!

The choices available to service users and their carers will be very dependent upon the ability of agencies to collaborate with one another on service developments. But these developments will not be effective unless they address, in a relevant way, the needs which are uncovered through the care management process. Developmental units will thus need good links with care managers, service providers and service users/carers. Developmental work will need to feed into service contracting arrangements and if, as seems likely, 'service menus' are put together, not by individual care managers but by others, the links between these three groups will be of great significance.

All parts of the community care system need to be 'quality assured'. This means that the criteria set for specific bits of the system need to complement one another and there needs to be a way of ensuring that all those involved in all parts of the system feed back to one another. Therefore service monitoring cannot just consist of specific input/output measures (DOH/SSI, 1991a, pp.69–70). It also has to consist of ways of evaluating the part played by the service in the overall community care system. This can only be done if information is shared and discussions are opened up through a quality assurance partnership.

Management support cannot just mean the direct support of workers. It has also to mean that managers liaise with their opposite numbers in other units, divisions or agencies while simultaneously building supportive structures for their own workers. Training has to draw upon the experiences of care managers, service providers, service users and their carers and has to be linked to the processes of service development in order to ensure that it is relevant and useful.

Increasingly, all those involved with the development of community care will have to look towards models of partnership in order to develop 'plural, yet integrated, systems of care management' (DOH/SSI, 1991a, p.74). There has been an increasing recognition that the development of a 'seamless' community care service will depend in large part on the effectiveness of 'lead managers' (DOH/SSI, 1991b, p.22), but in order to really grasp partnership opportunities these 'lead managers' should be allowed to operate not just as inter-agency negotiators but as brokers facilitating and coordinating a number of wide-ranging partnerships between service users, carers, professionals and agencies in order to create the kind of culture within which case management and service delivery can be effective.

Community care is not unique. We need to recognise that partnership systems of all kinds will grow in importance in future years and as they do so they will raise questions of coordination and integration which can only be addressed if there are specific individuals who are enabled to conceive their role in networking terms. This raises interesting questions not just about community care but also about the whole nature of management in the new social services world. If managers are to be networkers, this suggests that the key management task may increasingly be the management of the negotiating process.

Community brokerage in practice

Given everything that has been said about the way in which the delivery of present-day social welfare services depends on various types of brokerage, the reader might be forgiven for thinking that what has been described is a common feature of practice. But the findings of the North London Project suggest that its presence should not be taken for granted. In a letter to those participating, the project defined brokerage very generally as 'the activity of going between different agencies or professional groups with the aim of bringing them closer together' and went on to emphasise that it was 'less concerned with "one off" forms of brokerage which are specifically concerned with the delivery of services' than with more general roles.

In the event, although the project found plenty of evidence for partnership and liaison, there was little evidence of the kind of activity which could be called systems brokerage. One reason for this was that individual practitioners tended to develop very personalised and individualised networks which were not available to other members of their own organisations. Another, more deep-seated, reason might be the difficulty many of those taking part had in perceiving the benefits of anything which did not produce immediate and identifiable outcomes. Helping other organisations to work more effectively with one another falls, almost by definition, outside this conceptual framework (Trevillion, 1996a).

Even where there is a strong belief in the value of 'cooperation', brokerage activities are often designed to ensure that specific individuals receive an appropriate range of services, rather than establishing new links between different agencies (Trevillion and Green, 1998). To the extent that I have found evidence of a willingness to invest in long-term relationship building between teams and organisations, the focus has almost always been on the links an individual or team could build for itself, rather than on the construction of a set of linkages between the different participants. Where these links have developed it has been by accident and without any real planning.

In network terms, what appears to be happening is that a loose-knit network is put together, focused on a particular individual or team, and which may have little durability as a result. While systems brokerage is the logical extension of other forms of brokerage, there appear to be significant barriers to its development. While it is not possible to investigate these barriers in depth here, their presence needs to be acknowledged and, if networking is to fully realise its potential, they need to be overcome.

5 Inter-agency networking

The problem of collaboration

Inter-agency work has long been seen as the key to primary health care (Kleizkowski *et al.*, 1984, p.16). More recently, it has been mooted that this should also encompass strategic linkages between health and social care (Duggan, 1995). Arguments for a multi-agency approach have been made for even longer in relation to child protection (Maher, 1987, pp.145–7) and whole areas of policy making such as community care and child care have now become linked to the ability of the health, housing and social services to work together (Lewis and Glennerster, 1996, p.165; DOH, 1991, s.1.8). Even urban regeneration has come to be seen as dependent on the existence of a 'networking organisation' (Macfarlane and Laville, 1992, p.111).

But there is always a danger not only of proposing inadequate or inappropriate solutions, but also of misunderstanding the nature of the problem of collaboration. The recent literature on the 'health and social care divide' tends to assume that the problem of collaboration consists either of inadequate or insufficient guidance from central government, unclear agency and professional boundaries leading to role confusion or persistent cultural differences generating constant conflict and misunderstanding between health and social services. While these ideas may appear to be superficially attractive, they lead to 'top down' solutions which often make the problem worse (Trevillion, 1996b, pp.11–14).

The plea for more guidance tends to lead to requests for more centralised direction and control. The focus on boundary maintenance may lead to a clearer division of labour, but it does nothing to encourage individuals or organisations to question their assumptions or explore new ways of working together. Finally, the concept of cultural differences tends to define the problem of collaboration as irrational resistance to progress and this in turn suggests 'solutions' which often consist of management seeking to impose new organisational and professional values from the top down. While managers and policy makers need to define the overall aims and create an enabling context for inter-agency work, their efforts may be self-defeating if they lead to rigid and stereotypical forms of the division of professional labour and only partially successful attempts to force people to change their values and beliefs. While good organisation and effective administration will always be essential, if these are to be delivered through interorganisational networks then more attention will need to be paid to network processes than has hitherto been the case.

Contrary to much of the received wisdom on the subject (for example, Payne, 1986b), inter-agency collaboration is much less about the way in which organisations gradually merge into one another to create new organisations than it is about the restructuring of organisational life itself on network principles. Some of this has already been touched on, but if we are witnessing the birth of new, open-ended, social networks criss-crossing the spaces between organisations and creating a new interorganisational space characterised by new patterns of 'connectedness' (Statham, 1996), this is the context in which we should be discussing inter-agency work.

In the general context of networking in which there is always a strong emphasis on making links across organisational boundaries, how easy is it to separate inter-agency work from any other type of networking? One of the most commonly used definitions of inter-agency work stresses that it should involve 'joint initiatives' (Hall, 1988, p.82). But what exactly is a 'joint initiative' and how can this be defined so as to avoid the trap of making inter-agency work synonymous with almost any example of networking? It seems right to insist that inter-agency work must be focused on more than a particular short-term problem of service delivery. On the other hand, given the criticisms already made about an overreliance on 'top down' decision making, it also seems appropriate to define 'joint' or collective 'initiatives' in such a way that practitioners as well as managers can be seen to play an active part.

Inter-agency work might be expected to have two distinct outcomes, both of which need to be incorporated into any definition of inter-agency networking. There needs to be some process of collective decision making, but there also needs to be a discernible impact on the relationship between the participating organisations. This produces the following definition:

Inter-agency networking is the development and maintenance of a system of interorganisational linkage characterised by collective decision making and a set of positive feedback relationships between the internal structure, systems and values of participating organisations and the interorganisational network of which they are all members.

This suggests that it is possible to distinguish conceptually between the inter-agency network and the agencies themselves. This may seem curious, but in practice this separation is easy to observe as the set of inter-agency linkages is usually managed by a relatively small set of key individuals drawn from the participating organisations.

Take your partners?

Many inter-agency partnerships are based upon a shared interest and involvement with a particular client group. Community mental handicap teams, for example, operate as multidisciplinary networks of social workers, nurses, psychologists, speech therapists and so on, seeking to coordinate service delivery (Humphreys and McGrath, 1986). But the process of deciding which agencies to link up with is not always straightforward. Should only specialist organisations be included, or should more general welfare organisations which devote a considerable amount of time to the client group also be invited to participate? Should user groups be included, and how might the interests of families and carers best be represented?

Even relatively narrowly defined client groups may raise issues like this. The joint planning teams set up as a forum to discuss issues relating to the care of people with HIV and AIDS were meant to include representatives from health and social services, but also representatives from voluntary organisations. But which ones? No clear answers to this question were ever devised and the membership of joint planning teams varied as a result.

The purchaser/provider split associated with the NHS and Community Care Act has created new kinds of problems for inter-agency work. This can be seen in relation to the difficulties now being encountered with 'joint commissioning'. It has been widely assumed that relations between the commissioning partners (health and social services) and the service providers can be governed purely by market-led considerations and detailed contractual arrangements, but this can lead to problems, for example, in relation to hospital discharge arrangements, about which complaints have multiplied in recent years. According to an Age Concern spokesperson:

Health purchasers are not based in hospitals and as a result communication between purchasers and providers is often poor. Trusts don't purchase services so, unless collaboration is good, service users may not get the district nurse they need or equipment such as incontinence supplies. (*Community Care*, 1997, p.19)

Partnership clearly needs to extend across the purchaser/provider divide, but if there is an attempt to do this, it is again not always clear who should be included and who excluded. Moreover, the range and diversity of provider organisations (Taylor *et al.*, 1995) may pose problems for any attempt to impose a common set of expectations on all partners. If this were not enough, there can be conflicts between the demands of the joint commissioning partnership and the broader partnership embracing both purchasers and providers.

The need to involve service users and local communities at the planning and commissioning stage also raises some difficult questions. Should all those living in a particular local or health authority area have some say in these matters? As this is likely to prove impossible, should the emphasis be on those currently using services? The latter may simplify the process of identifying partners, but if one of the problems is the low level of service delivery to certain parts of the community such as black and ethnic minority groups, then focusing exclusively on existing service user groups might make matters worse.

Choosing a locality focus does not always resolve these difficulties either. What of agencies equally active in more than one locality? As each agency is likely to define its geographical boundaries somewhat differently, which definition should be adopted as the boundary of the inter-agency network? Sometimes, differences of organisational culture ensure that these issues remain unresolved.

When I worked in a neighbourhood-based social work team in London I found that health service representatives persisted in treating what I saw as an inter-agency 'patch' network, with a number of different partners, as a link between the health service and the local authority as a whole, which effectively ignored not only other neighbourhood-based organisations but also the local social work team.

The introduction of Health Action Zones is an attempt to solve these problems by 'developing locality commissioning' in wide-ranging partnerships within a common, clearly defined geographical territory (Peck and Poxton, 1998, p.7).

In addition to the key agencies responsible for implementing collective decisions, there will also be a wider network of stakeholders. This poses a problem which is not just practical but also ethical and philosophical, because the stakeholder argument is essentially a moral and political one. In principle, it suggests that all those who have a 'stake' in the outcome of a decision should be involved in making that decision. Does this mean that any inter-agency network should also include representatives of the stakeholder network? It may complicate decision making but it will also add to the legitimacy and acceptability of decision making.

The West London Project showed that a wide range of stakeholders could come together to make decisions and, according to its co-director, the London Health Partnership appears similarly to have found little difficulty in working with a mixed service agency and stakeholder network:

> Work with local partnerships begins with a burning local issue, such as how to improve hospital discharge, how to stop lonely deaths, or how to avoid last year's winter bed crisis. First, we engage stakeholders who bring together people representing the whole community of interest around their burning issue.
>
> Then the LHP designs custom-made conferences which allow local players to find common ground they are prepared to work for. Participants range from those at the top to those at the bottom of organisations and great care is taken to ensure they are not just the usual suspects. The events take place over two or three days and generate a range of actions by local people. These are different in each place. After this, we look at the implementation and learning how to sustain the changes. (*Community Care*, 1997, p.21)

Linking stakeholder and service agency networks can be successful provided that the process is carefully managed and attention is paid to the creation of a consensus. The fact that irreconcilable differences are not mentioned suggests that, perhaps, areas of 'common ground' will always be found if there is enough commitment to finding them.

Brokers and representatives

As we saw in Chapter 4, there are many examples of inter-agency networks which depend on specific brokers. Community care is a notable example of what I have called 'systems brokerage'. However, not all inter-agency networks fall into this category. Brokers tend to be associated with those initiatives where a particular agency is primarily responsible for the success of an initiative. In the case of community care, local authorities have been identified as the 'lead agency' and it is therefore not surprising to find that they sometimes take on the role of 'systems broker'. However, even within the broad context of community care, some issues are likely to be driven forward by other agencies as much as by social services departments.

A close look at the work of the London Health Partnership shows that issues such as hospital discharge may be a matter of such grave concern to so many organisations that it would be false to describe the process of establishing a partnership as dependent on one particular agency acting as a broker. All those involved actively seek to represent their issues and concerns. The reality is that everyone is active and everyone networks with everyone else. Networks like this might be best described as representative networks, in that each agency is actively represented and the representatives as a whole manage the partnership system.

As with any other kind of networking, inter-agency networking operates at a number of different levels simultaneously and what follows applies equally to those networks based on specific brokers and those consisting of linked representatives.

The interpersonal network within an inter-agency network

Inter-agency links are too easily seen in depersonalised terms. All the inter-agency projects in which I have been involved have relied on a relatively small number of committed individuals as well as the broader support of their respective organisations. These include GP/social worker liaisons undertaken in the period 1981–3, a network of local organisations supporting the work of a community interpreting service during the same period, a forum for agencies representing the interests of older people in the period 1984–6, a broad-based patch network representing ten different local agencies who met regularly for a 'patch lunch' at a community centre in the period 1984–5 and, more recently, a large Diploma in Social Work Programme network consisting of more than 20 statutory and voluntary organisations from all over London. Although all of these networks have been very different, they have all shared this feature of conducting organisational business in an informal manner through individuals who have often got to know one another very well.

In some situations, the potential sensitivity of some inter-agency linkages may mean that all communication needs to be channelled through specific individuals nominated by participating agencies. When setting up GP/social work liaisons as a neighbourhood social worker, I found that even the most welcoming and interested GPs insisted on channelling all their communications through specific named individuals. Thereafter, these liaisons seemed to work best when there were regular meetings between the named social workers and the GPs. Looking back on this now, it seems to me that the key issue here was trust. Because networking takes place out-side established procedures, it involves an element of risk taking and, in a situation where trust may in any case be very fragile (Hunter and Wistow, 1987, p.140) and there is always a danger of 'inter-professional demarcation disputes' breaking out (Hill, 1982, p.73), these risks only become acceptable if bonds of personal trust can be developed.

The same principles appear to apply at higher management levels.

In the course of a group discussion which formed part of the West London Project, a social services manager talked about a network of managers from different agencies which he attended on a regular basis. He made a point of emphasising that one of the most important elements in the success of this venture was the way it had enabled personal relationships to flourish. As a result, where issues could be routed in a predictable way through named managers, problems could generally be solved with a minimum of conflict. However, this led him to express concern about how well the inter-agency system could deal with emergencies. Unpredictable situations which obliged individuals who did not know one another to solve problems quite often produced conflicts and tensions and in these situations the inter-agency liaison network seemed to be of little help.

Where inter-agency work is successful, it seems to demonstrate that it is not agencies which relate to one another but people representing agencies. Where large-scale bureaucratic organisations are concerned, a constant and skilled brokerage effort is frequently needed to prevent the breakdown of the inter-agency network. Helping staff to manage their inter-agency rela-tionships has been compared with the work of marriage guidance counsel-lors: 'Those lucky managers charged with running joint health and social services projects have, like counsellors from Relate, beavered away behind the scenes, working for a nearly perfect marriage where staff from both sides strive together to offer clients a seamless service' (*Community Care*, 1997, p. 19).

The inter-agency network as a 'task community'

One of the aims of inter-agency networking is to generate a sense of collec-tive commitment to collective decisions. This is not easy.

In one case, a social worker whom I was supervising gained the rather passive agreement of her team to undertake liaison work with the home care team. Having successfully negotiated an opportunity for social workers to meet specific home helps by appointment at a fixed time of the week, she was dismayed to discover that few social workers were willing to make use of this opportunity. It needed much subsequent work and continual 'reminders' to her colleagues to increase the number making use of the new liaison possibilities.

This kind of problem occurs when the interpersonal nature of the decision-making network leads to the development of an inter-agency clique out of touch with the feelings of the colleagues they are supposed to represent. This creates a tension between the tendency for the members of a strongly committed decision-making or representative network to become closely identified with one another and the dangers this poses of a split between inter-agency structures and the participating organisations.

As any inter-agency network has to be judged by the results it achieves, these kinds of problems need to be taken seriously and we should avoid assuming that an effective and well organised 'task community' is always a very close-knit structure. Some degree of 'connectedness' is essential, but an overly 'dense' inter-agency network may prove to be counterproductive if it excludes others. One answer to these kinds of problems is to ensure that everybody in an organisation gets a chance to participate in an inter-agency network.

The neighbourhood social work team in which I worked in the period 1981–4 was involved with other similar teams from the same local authority in regular meetings to learn from one another's experiences and to undertake shared 'policy' making. The meeting rotated through the different patch offices and was very much a collective responsibility.

This is an example of a close-knit inter-agency network which managed to avoid the problem of cliques by including everybody. However, this kind of solution is only possible on a very small scale.

One of the tests of an effective task community is external to the service agencies themselves and that is the extent to which the community is open to the wider stakeholder network discussed earlier on and to particular service users. An inter-agency 'community' cannot be said to exist if service users, the 'citizens' of that 'community' are excluded from it. Therefore structures need to be developed for opening out inter-agency links to user involvement, and not just on agency terms. As Croft and Beresford remind us, people want 'more control over their own lives' and this involves playing a genuine role in the inter-agency decision-making process, a process which involves moving from a preoccupation with 'personal troubles to collective policy' (Croft and Beresford, 1989, p.16).

Flexibility and accountability

There is a conflict between the bureaucratic mode of organisation and inter-agency networking. A classical bureaucracy encourages vertical communication up and down the various management levels and this has an impact on the transmission of information (Weber, 1978, pp.956–1005). Few organisations correspond precisely to this ideal type. Local authorities for example, are, influenced strongly by non-bureaucratic factors such as local politics, and yet there is a tendency towards bureaucracy in most large organisations. The concept of a 'networking organisation' is probably as much of an ideal type as the concept of a 'bureaucracy'. Few organisations correspond precisely to the expectations one might have of a 'networking organisation' and yet, where networking is found, it tends to encourage horizontal communication across organisational boundaries rather than vertical communication within organisational boundaries. Where bureaucracy and networking coexist (as they usually do) this tension can cause problems.

Networking undermines bureaucratic power and it calls into question rules or assumptions which have never before been called into question and which have helped to define organisational 'culture' (Schein, 1985). In doing so, it can create an institutional 'backlash'. One of the interprofessional discussion groups which were a feature of the West London Project discussed this issue in some depth.

Almost all members of the group felt that managers could feel threatened by the 'participative' and 'democratic' characteristics of inter-agency networking and they related this to the fact that all their organisations were still quite hierarchical. But there was also a general acknowledgement that their organisations recognised that networking could be helpful. On the whole they tended to the view that their organisations were becoming more 'network-friendly' than in the past but that more traditional attitudes still survived. This group also identified somewhat inadvertently one of the key problems for organisations seeking to become more 'network-friendly'.

This group, which did not include any managers, were unanimous in their view that the best managers were those who simply set a broad context and resource framework and then left workers to do what they thought most appropriate in relation to inter-agency work.

But if, by definition, inter-agency work is work done on behalf of one's own agency, it is not clear how this kind of individualised decision making could possibly deliver a genuine inter-agency arrangement. These comments suggest a lack of clarity about the difference between interprofessional collaboration on problems of service delivery and interorganisational linkage.

There is an echo of this theme in the results of the North London Project. In some ways these seemed to represent the ideal situation described by the professionals in the other project. Interprofessional linkages were highly individualised and there was little or no sense of management interference in the way these relationships were conducted, but the result was a lack of interorganisational linkages even at a team level (Trevillion, 1996a, p.98).

While flexibility and informality are the hallmarks of inter-agency networking, achieving them at the expense of organisational fragmentation is clearly counterproductive, as there appears to be little point in developing linkages between organisations if these organisations cannot make corporate decisions. There has to be accountability and there has to be some measure of control. How is this to be achieved?

In part, the answer may be to focus as much on intra-agency linkages as on inter-agency linkages and to ensure that, however informal the style of work, there are clear channels of communication and accountability within the teams, sections and organisations that networkers represent. If parts of a particular organisation become so closely engaged with other organisations that they start to develop new interorganisational identities then this needs to be formally acknowledged and linked to new mechanisms capable of delivering effective communication and accountability, perhaps by adopting some of the procedures and processes associated with stakeholder networks.

Networking the communication system

In some respects, it is very artificial to try to separate a discussion about inter-agency communication networks from the debates about appropriate types of linkage and ways of using linkages to promote shared or collaborative working. In a sense, an effective communication network is simply one which enables these kind of inter-agency processes to occur. In addition, much of what has already been said about promoting network awareness and acting as an 'interpreter' applies as much to inter-agency work as to any other kind of networking and community brokerage. But it is probably worth taking the risk of sounding repetitive to state clearly that inter-agency cooperation cannot flourish unless there is a shared understanding of key issues.

A social services department may be seeking to implement a policy of removing suspected abusers rather than their victims from households in which abuse has taken place. But to do this they need cooperation from the housing department. If the issue is seen as giving abusers priority over other people on the housing waiting list, it is likely that there will be considerable resistance to the idea both from the housing department and from those housing associations which specialise in accommodation for single people.

Prior to any formal request for cooperation with a policy of removing abusers, representatives of all these agencies should meet to explore the issues together and formulate a policy to which they could all feel committed. This process will probably be much more effective if incest survivors or mothers desperate to keep their children out of care have some opportunity for participating in these discussions and making their views known.

It is often a specific issue like this which, because it cannot be resolved easily, leads agencies to invest time in their relationships with one another. In doing so, they often discover a number of other issues which can be talked about informally. Communication channels set up to discuss the issue of rehousing abusers can also be used for discussing the position of homeless families in particular hotels, or elderly people who become homeless as a result of family disputes. If the discussions extend to the position of people recently discharged from psychiatric hospital and placed in bed and breakfast hotels, the partnership might invite representatives of the health authority to join. In this way the communication network might continue to grow and evolve over time.

There is no one ideal pattern of inter-agency communication, but, on the basis of all the issues which have so far been raised, it would seem as if networkers trying to develop appropriate channels of communication should ensure the following:

- the flow of information across the interorganisational interface is managed by a relatively small number of people who know one another well;
- information flowing through these inter-agency information brokers is transmitted to and from a range of clearly identified strategically positioned individuals and groups within the broker/representative's own agency;
- communication links between service agency and stakeholder networks are established and maintained, and these links are fully integrated with consultative and decision-making systems;
- the growth of the communication network is paced appropriately over time.

Mobilising resources

An inter-agency action set is a network of agencies involved in some form of collaboration. Almost always, these same agencies will have established liaison relationships with one another. In order to understand the inter-agency action set process, we need to understand the relationship between liaison and collaboration and, as a first step, we need to define our terms.

The words 'liaison' and 'collaboration' are sometimes used interchangeably, as if they had the same meaning, but it is probably best to see them as referring to different aspects of inter-agency partnership. It has been argued that they refer to different degrees or levels of partnership. In this view, organisations can be seen as moving through a number of 'stages' in their relationship with one another from 'communication', through 'cooperation' and 'coordination' to 'federation' (Payne, 1986b, p.75). But this model is questionable because a high level of organisational integration, perhaps rather surprisingly, does not in itself seem necessarily to produce an effective mobilisation of inter-agency resources.

The work of Community Mental Handicap Teams (CMHTs), in at least some areas, appears to have been undermined by the lack of understanding and ability to work together of the NHS and local authority social services (Humphreys and McGrath, 1986, pp.21–7) even though the teams themselves were organisationally integrated, corresponding to Payne's concept of a 'federative stage' of development. The CMHT experience suggests that, rather than seeing liaison and collaboration as different 'stages' or 'levels' of networking, it may be better to see liaison as embodying the continuity of contact between agencies which is essential to the success of collaborative initiatives. In terms of network theory, liaison can then be thought of in terms of the development of action set 'potential', and collaboration as the process of mobilising an action set. Likewise effective network communication may not be simply the first stage of community partnership but rather the process which underpins the future of the relationship as well.

This may help us to distinguish between genuine liaison and activities which may be described as such but which do not create action set potential. The North London Project provides some good examples of this difference between rhetoric and reality.

John Smith is a HIV social worker. He is based in a social services department team but has a lot of contact with health professionals and medical charities. Superficially, his involvement in inter-agency work appears to be impressive. Not only does he have a large number of inter-agency contacts but he also clearly identifies liaison with other agencies as a key role. In fact he has intensive contact with ten organisations and, of the ten areas of activity into which he divides his work, two specifically relate to liaison work. But, if we explore these liaison activities in more depth, a number of less reassuring features emerge. Not one of the ten organisations with whom he has most frequent contact figures in his liaison activities. Even more surprisingly, none of those individuals with whom he has the most intensive contact actively participates in his liaison work.

What is notable about this is not the relatively low level of interactions devoted exclusively to liaison but the lack of any obvious relationship between liaison and mainstream service delivery work. When statistical tests were applied to these features at a team level, they confirmed this impression of the marginality of liaison (Trevillion, 1996a, pp.99–100). While it would be very rash to conclude that John Smith, or even his team, is in some way a typical example of contemporary inter-agency work, what this piece of research does show is that it is very easy to be misled by appearances and to assume that activities which are described as 'liaison' actually make a difference to service delivery, when the opposite may be true.

Inter-agency 'rules' and 'contracts'

The history of the CMHTs and of joint planning and joint finance (Hunter and Wistow, 1987, pp.110–56) suggests that local authorities and health authorities may not be able to work well with each other in the absence of clear 'partnership contracts'. Underlying this, perhaps, is the problem of joint 'ownership'. Liaison links can be used to work out the basis of a future collaboration. The issues which the partnership contract will need to address will depend on the nature of the collaboration.

A contract for an inter-agency project such as a CMHT will need to pay attention to issues such as accountability and line management responsibilities, the resources which will be committed to the project by the various agencies, the proportion of time to be devoted to service delivery, as opposed to developmental work, and confidentiality. The purpose of such a contract is to support workers and give them the confidence to develop new ways of working, rather than to impose a new bureaucracy, and it is important that this principle is respected, otherwise the contract will be disabling rather than enabling. But contracts like this can never be negotiated once and for all.

I remember from my own experience the case of an inter-agency 'rule' which obliged social workers to inform health visitors of any child care concerns or of any new families with young children moving into the area. This rule was constantly flouted by social workers. The health visitors communicated their concern but nothing happened. Discussion within the social work team revealed that people were either unfamiliar with this 'rule' or unhappy about it because it appeared to conflict with the professional 'rules' about confidentiality. Eventually a new inter-agency code of conduct was negotiated which took account of confidentiality and which was respected.

Where inter-agency collaboration is to be directed more towards strategic planning than to a specific project, the contract will need to address a different set of issues. A community care planning partnership may need to involve a social services department, a housing department, a health authority, a number of voluntary organisations, service users and carers. In order to do business with one another they will need to develop a shared understanding of issues such as the roles they are expecting one another to play and the power of the partnership to make decisions which will be binding on all its members.

One of the secrets of developing and then maintaining an effective inter-agency action set is coordination. But the most appropriate way of coordinating a particular inter-agency partnership will depend on the situation. One issue is the size of the network. If it is not too big, it may be a good idea to call a network meeting. If a liaison relationship between social workers, community workers, a tenants' association and a local church-based group revealed a need for a new youth club on an estate where territorial rivalries effectively made other clubs inaccessible to local young people, a network meeting might enable the partnership to begin work on a campaign to persuade others that a new club was absolutely essential.

The meeting could divide key tasks between different agencies. The community workers might gather and collate evidence of the need and present it to officers and members of the local authority. The social workers might write their own reports, commenting on the need for preventative services on an estate with high rates of juvenile crime and on young people being 'looked after' or coming into 'care'. The church-based group and the tenants' association might contact the local media and persuade them to run stories about the lives of local youngsters and lobby local politicians about the strength of feeling on the estate in support of the campaign. Some network members might seek to broaden the base of the campaign by involving local young people themselves, the police and the probation service. Subsequent meetings could review strategy and develop the campaign as it went along.

Sometimes the inter-agency network will be too complex to enable mobilisation of resources to be undertaken through a single planning meeting. The development of a mental health resource centre might need to be undertaken by a number of specialist groups, each one concerned with a particular service. For example, the drop-in centre might be developed by community psychiatric nurses, a volunteer organiser and social workers from local patch teams together with service users, whereas advice and information services might need to be developed by the Citizens' Advice Bureau and community workers. In a situation like this, it might be advisable to appoint an overall network coordinator who would act as a broker 'interweaving' the different groups into a viable whole. But network coordinators are not managers and if they possess authority it is only because all those involved are prepared to vest some authority in them.

A way forward?

This chapter has drawn attention to a number of problems and difficulties as well as a number of key principles. We have seen, for example, that patterns of interaction between individuals from different agencies can occur without producing any inter-agency collaboration. It may not be possible to say whether the results will be good or bad, but what is obvious is that such networks will develop without any overall sense of strategic direction and may carry all those involved, including the users of services, off into uncharted and potentially dangerous territory.

Inter-agency work has to be carried out on behalf of an organisation, not an individual, and it must be oriented towards achieving the strategic objectives of individual organisations, not the whims and fancies of individuals, however creative they might be. This implies careful attention to the way in which patterns of communication are organised, clear structures of accountability and the appropriate use of contracts, as well as the encouragement of creativity and informality. This is not an easy combination for any organisation or set of organisations to deliver and so it is not surprising that the problem of collaboration has proved so difficult to solve. Nevertheless, networking perspectives provide a framework with which to guide practitioners and managers in this difficult area.

6   Care management revisited

The alchemists of welfare

Care management was developed many years ago in the USA and Canada, where it is still known as 'case management'. By the early 1980s, its two key characteristics had already been identified. Austin had described it as 'a mechanism for linking and coordinating segments of a service delivery system (within a single agency or involving several providers)' (Austin, 1983, p.16). This captures the way in which case or care management is an attempt to ensure that services are delivered in an integrated fashion and that diversity and complexity do not lead to fragmentation, inefficiency and confusion. Meanwhile Steinberg and Carter had coined the now familiar term 'service' or 'care packages' and emphasised that these 'packages' had to be developed on the basis of an understanding of the needs of particular individuals (Steinberg and Carter, 1984, p.xi), thereby capturing one of the key paradoxes of case or care management, the attempt to define individual need in holistic terms while seeking to meet it through a variety of highly differentiated specialist services.

Putting these two early definitions together, we can see that care management is less a technical or mechanistic device than it is an aspiration. It aspires to an ideal world in which 'real' need is both understood and met in holistic terms, but it operates in a far from perfect everyday world of rival professions, organisational conflict and scarcity of resources. Care packaging or service coordination is the way in which care management tries to reconcile what is ultimately irreconcilable. As a result, care management is, perhaps, doomed to perpetually frustrate all those involved with it because its aims can never be finally realised. This does not mean, however, that it

103

should be dismissed as a failure. The mediaeval alchemists may have been wrong to believe that 'base' metals could be transformed into gold, but their failures laid the basis of modern chemistry. Likewise, care managers can be seen as the alchemists of modern welfare, constantly seeking to transform inadequate resources and inappropriate services into the philosopher's stone of a genuinely needs-led service. The philosopher's stone, of course, lies forever beyond their grasp, but it will be the contention of this chapter that, if they base their work on networking principles, they will frequently discover quite new and unexpectedly successful ways of working with complex situations.

Care management in practice

The early years of care management in the UK were characterised by a high level of confusion as to what it actually was (Lewis and Glennerster, 1996) but, as some of this early confusion has receded, a number of more distinct problems have begun to emerge. Some are related to inter-agency work, some are related to problems of empowerment, some are related to the shortage of resources for community care, in particular, and social care, in general; but there is one problem which goes to the heart of care management and that is its apparent failure to deliver a genuinely needs-led community care system.

Although the philosophy of care management is that a person should receive a unique blend of services reflecting his or her own unique needs, there is considerable evidence of a tendency to standardise both services and procedures. Suggesting that 'the introduction of assessment and care management has not benefited people with learning disabilities', Smith argues that this is rooted in the drive towards uniformity: 'Most authorities have been obsessed with creating uniform procedures to meet the needs of all client groups and particularly elderly people. In doing this they have lost some of the unique features needed to meet the individual needs of people with learning disabilities (Smith, 1995, p.7). In general, it seems that individuals are still made to fit services, rather than the other way around. Dipping into Greek mythology to make this point, Ritchie suggests that 'the tradition of tailoring in services owes more to Procrustes than to Savile Row' (Ritchie, 1994, p.133). While no system of welfare can hope to operate fairly and equitably without reference to some common standards, and individual claims will always need to be considered within the broader context of public priorities, these concerns go deeper.

One of the three key aims of the community care legislation was to 'give people a greater individual say in how they live their lives and the services they need to help them to do so' (Cm 849, s.1.8) and this was supposed to lead to 'services that respond flexibly and sensitively to the needs of individuals and their 'carers' (ibid., s.1.10). But care management, in practice, is now frequently accused of leading to an 'increase in bureaucracy' which appears to have accompanied the new procedures to the extent that 'the formalisation of procedures threatens to change the nature of social work practice' (Lewis *et al.*, 1997, p. 22). Rather than achieving a flowering of creativity, care management has, all too frequently, it seems, led to a move away from a professional culture and towards a 'managerial culture' (Lewis and Glennerster, 1996, p.143). And so it is argued that care management is implicated in turning activities at one time shaped by professional judgement into a '(semi) mechanical process' involving 'production line' techniques 'de-skilling' workers and turning them into 'slavish followers of protocols, devised not by themselves as part of a culture of good practice, but as set by those who want to control them as they themselves are controlled' (Simic, 1995, pp.13–14).

The increasing recognition that there is a problem associated with the tendency towards standardisation rather than individualisation has created a new orthodoxy which regards care management as irreconcilably opposed to social work and indeed any kind of person-centred human service activity. Simic speaks for many when he writes: 'The interpersonal features of practice that many associated with social work are disappearing in deadline and throughput dominated practice' (ibid., p.12). This is a powerful argument, persuasively put and while it is not the fundamental 'linking' and 'coordinating' principles of care management which are responsible for the general move towards market competition, contract-based relationships and the refusal of central government to take any responsibility for defining the relationship between 'rights', 'needs' and services in conditions of scarcity (Trevillion, 1996d), there must now be serious doubt about the extent to which current models of care management can refocus attention on the relationships with service uses, carers and other professionals which are supposed to underpin both the assessment process (Cm 849, ss.3.2.4–3.2.6) and the process of care planning (ibid., s.3.3.1). This is exemplified by the problems associated with operationalising the idea of 'partnership'.

The gap between rhetoric and reality

As part of the North London Project, 11 social workers, the entire membership of two teams of social workers/care managers (six members of a specialist HIV team and five members of a mental health team), were interviewed and asked what the concept of 'partnership' meant to them. The aim of this was not to be able to generalise about care managers' attitudes but rather to compare attitudes and practices within the context of a particular organisation at a particular time.

Ten of the responses demonstrated a strong awareness of the relationship base of effective partnership arrangements. Themes such as 'trust' and 'mutual understanding' were present in almost all the responses. Even the one respondent who was sceptical about partnership acknowledged that an effort had to be made to develop good working relationships. However, when these general statements were compared with the statements which the same people made about specific 'partnerships', the gap between rhetoric and reality was striking.

There was little evidence in the study of any deliberate attempt to develop relationships and it was hard to avoid the conclusion that in practice the term 'partnership' was defined on the basis of three features which had little or nothing to do with the themes of 'trust' or 'mutual understanding' which were such a feature of the general definitions they had given. These were instrumentality (there was a strong association between problem solving and partnership), intensity (high frequencies of interaction were positively associated with partnership) and durability (the concept of partnership was only applied to relatively long-term relationships).

It is hard for care managers to practise what they preach. While these care managers were involved with networks of service providers, this did not mean that attention was being given to developing or sustaining patterns of linkage. The result was that, in contrast to initial assessment and the process of putting together 'care packages', opportunities for actively working alongside others were very limited. In some respects, the situation seemed to exemplify Simic's point about 'throughput dominated practice'.

Some of the reasons for this may have been quite local. The comments made by one of the team leaders seemed to suggest that the fragmentation of work at the care management level was duplicated throughout the organisation, with very little attention being paid to support and coordination. However, the 'fit' between this picture and that of some of the general comments which have been made about care management by its critics is too close to ignore. Is this kind of pattern inevitable or is a fresh relationship-oriented approach possible?

A fresh approach?

We have known for many years that the 'packaging' of care is dependent on an ability to work with clients and 'informal carers' (Steinberg and Carter, 1984, pp.25–6) as well as with representatives of other agencies. In fact, the relationship tradition in care management goes back to the 'interweaving' strategies advocated originally in the 1968 Seebohm Report and subsequently elaborated upon in the 1982 Barclay Report under the rubric of 'community social work'. It has also been known for some time that the careful stitching together of relationships and the work needed to ensure that those relationships remain robust and enduring are critically dependent on 'face-to-face' communication and negotiation with clients and carers (Bayley, 1973, pp.316–17).

As these principles are so well established and as care managers themselves often appear to subscribe to them, why has it proved so difficult to incorporate them successfully in care management practice? Part of the problem may lie with the concept of 'need' itself. While in some respects need is central to any form of care management, controversies and misunderstandings about what is meant by this term have tended to devalue the language of need to such an extent that it now appears either to embrace almost anything or to be associated with the way 'eligibility criteria' restrict access to a specified restricted range of health and social care services. Without jettisoning the idea of need altogether, it may now be time to re-evaluate it in the broader context of 'quality of life'.

It has been argued by some commentators that 'quality of life encompasses well-being in terms of both the inner self and the environment' and that plans based on a concern with 'quality of life' tend in any case to have better outcomes than those developed on the basis of other, more restricted criteria (Seed and Kaye, 1994, p.31). One of the other advantages it has is that it tends to focus less on the way in which specific needs can be met by specific services and more on the way a whole complex of linked issues, activities, services and relationships can contribute to 'well-being'. If one of the concerns about care management is with the way in which it has in some places been associated with a turning away from relationships, locating assessment, care planning and coordination within a 'quality of life' framework might help it to break away from the debilitating short-termism which has marred the early years of its development in the UK.

Some of the weaknesses of the dominant models of care management go back to its inception. The case management pioneers were so preoccupied with counteracting fragmentation that they oversimplified the relationship between control and coherence. Because of their concern with finding ways of taming the power of individual service providers and enforcing overall integration on behalf of the client, they neglected the problem of the overly powerful care manager and, even more fundamentally, they failed to explore the difference between setting up a resource system to enable specific services to be channelled to a relatively passive recipient and developing a network of potential resources to be actively deployed by the service user. By making a shift now, away from the former and towards the latter, we would also be making a shift away from the management of care services and towards a way of working closely with individuals to achieve an improved 'quality of life' by the active deployment of appropriate resources which might not always be formal services. This is a move away from conventional care management to what could be called 'brokering social support'.

It could be argued that this would still raise the same problems of finite resources and potentially unlimited demand as care management. As far as it goes, this is true. The concept of 'quality of life' does not create new resources (although it might lead to a more imaginative deployment of existing resources). However, what the concept does is to move the debate away from ways of restricting access to services by narrow 'eligibility criteria'. It focuses attention on the kind of rights which individuals in a society have to a way of life which is compatible with their status as citizens. This issue is explored in more depth in the next chapter, but the model of brokering social support which is proposed here would be dependent for its successful implementation on a willingness to move to a more clearly rights-based approach to social welfare.

Network approaches

There is some evidence that social network approaches are beginning to influence practice, albeit in a relatively intuitive way. For example, certain network themes kept recurring in the diaries which were kept by social workers/care managers as part of the West London Project.

Some key words such as 'support', 'facilitation' and 'co-ordination' were mentioned frequently. Some diaries also used specific phrases such as 'pulling together the network' and mention was made of a perceived connection between the quality of relationships in a support network and the effectiveness of the support provided.

While it was clear that those taking part in the West London Project often operated to tight deadlines and with a very short-term approach to problem solving, it was also clear that they sometimes acted quite differently. This can be understood in terms of the way in which they sometimes linked flexible and holistic approaches to definitions of 'need' with a willingness to think in network terms (Beresford and Trevillion, 1995, pp.43–4). However, the analysis can be taken a step further.

When operating in this particular mode or mind set, the care managers focused on network strengths ('a supportive family') and network opportunities ('access to transport') rather than problems and 'needs' and implicit within this was a concept of 'quality of life' even if this new language was not used by care managers themselves.

One of the advantages of trying to make these relational perspectives explicit is that it becomes possible to redefine care management as a certain kind of community brokerage.

Brokering support through the interpersonal domain

This aspect of brokering social support focuses on the way in which individual members of a support network are linked with one another and the impact of this on respect, reflexivity, reciprocity and 'connectedness'. The following case study is based on work undertaken by myself in the period 1982–3, which predates the community care reforms. It contains no references to purchasing, but it does contain many relational features which can be analysed in terms of the concept of 'brokerage'.

Emily Francombe is an 87-year-old woman. She lives alone in a bed-sit owned by a housing association. She is rather confused and very suspicious of others. She is convinced her neighbours are plotting against her and sometimes directly accuses them of this. Her mental and physical health continue to deteriorate until she stops paying her rent, regularly loses her pension book and sometimes goes without food for some days.

Having sent a representative to call on Emily Francombe who has not been allowed into the flat, the housing association make a referral to the social services department and a duty social worker tries to visit. She is also unsuccessful. Visits by other social workers and community psychiatric nurses fare no better. After each of these visits Emily Francombe complains to the neighbours who in their turn complain to the authorities, who respond by attempting to visit, which starts the cycle up, all over again. Things only start to improve when it is agreed that only one social worker should visit and that the housing association should cease trying to gain access to the flat. Eventually, this social worker gains access to the bed-sit and after several months manages to persuade her to accept a home help three times a week.

However, although Emily Francombe allows the home help to visit, she will not allow her to do any cleaning, only some minimal shopping; and if the home help is ill or on holiday, she refuses to allow any other home help into the flat. The social worker continues to visit but only every couple of weeks. When he does so, he becomes acutely aware of the additional anxieties generated by his presence and is forced to conclude that the day-to-day monitoring of the situation is, in any case, almost entirely dependent on the home help.

The general practitioner, social worker and community psychiatric nurse all agree that the home help should continue to visit Emily Francombe in spite of the limitations placed on her. But the home help has to cope with an enormous amount of stress as a result of these visits. Sometimes this elderly woman refuses to allow her into the bed-sit; sometimes she allows her in but cross-questions her about her movements; sometimes she subjects her to long lists of complaints about her neighbours and, because of her short-term memory loss, she almost always asks her the same questions over and over again. If the home help is to be enabled to continue her work she, herself, will need some help. The social worker decides that there is little point in visiting more frequently himself. Instead, he offers to see the home help for a regular consultation session, designed to provide the kind of additional support and assistance which would enable her to continue.

At first sight, it appears that the concept of 'quality of life' has little relevance here. However, the priorities of the professionals were determined by a willingness to try to find ways of helping Emily Francombe to lead the kind of life that she wanted and in that sense the whole strategy was predicated on a philosophy of 'choice'. Overall, this case study suggests that professional skills can sometimes be more effectively deployed supporting those doing the caring than in direct work.

At the outset, there is little sense of respectfulness. Emily Francombe feels intimidated by what to her appear to be confusing and suspicious encounters with various mysterious figures claiming some kind of official legitimacy. The neighbours feel intimidated by her and the professionals almost inevitably start to see her as a source of frustration and irritation, rather than as a very anxious and frightened person needing skilled help. While the interventions above could all be described in traditional case-work terms, it is also clear that this is a network crisis which is in danger of precipitating an urgent admission to hospital or residential care and that this is avoided by what could be called interpersonal brokerage.

Very few resources or care services are involved here. The work focuses on the way in which the linkages between key individuals are developed. As these linkages are reconceptualised and reorganised, there is a steady increase in 'respectfulness'. The social worker contributes to this by empa-thising with Emily Francombe's distress and seeking to reduce the disturb-ing and unpredictable aspects of her encounters with others to a minimum. Another way in which he does so is by recognising the very skilled work undertaken by the home help and creating a new kind of linkage between the two of them. In practical terms, this involves two strategic shifts in the network pattern. Regular consultation meetings between home help and social worker become a feature of the case and, at the same time, direct contact between the social worker and Emily Francombe is reduced to a minimum. These two changes are closely associated with one another as increased personal support for the home help is combined with an attempt to stop undermining her work by continuing to develop a separate relation-ship with someone who finds most social contacts very difficult to under-stand or accept.

There is another aspect of respect which is implicit in the case description but which should be made explicit. In order for the strategy of consultation to succeed, the potentially difficult relationship between the home help organiser and the social worker had to be carefully negotiated, so as to ensure that the line management responsibilities of the former did not conflict with the consultative role of the latter.

If we look at the sequence of events, it is clear that the decisions which help to promote respect are only made possible by reflexivity. These changes of direction are the result of considerable thought and reflection and each time they involve doing something unexpected. The first key decision in-volves allocating the case to one particular worker so as to break the spiral of numerous unknown professionals calling on Emily Francombe. The sec-ond turning point involves what, at first sight, looks like moving in an entirely different direction, quite inconsistent with the original decision to allocate the case to a named worker. Again, it might have been easy for a care manager who had worked hard to gain initial access to the flat to have persisted indefinitely with attempts to build a relationship with this elderly woman. Taking the decision to entrust direct work to the home help and focus on supporting her required a willingness to look afresh at the needs of the situation. Interpersonal brokerage therefore involves the ability to step back from the network process and to think about links and linkages in terms which are both strategic and empathic.

With someone as frail and confused as Emily Francombe, reciprocity may seem rather fanciful, but that is not to say it is completely absent from the network as a whole. The housing association agree to refrain from taking any action and to focus on supporting the neighbours. The neighbours are willing to contact the social worker if they are concerned about any problems, provided they feel someone is trying to help her. The home help is willing to undertake emotionally exhausting work, provided she receives help and advice from the social worker. The home help organiser is willing to accept a new and more demanding set of responsibilities for her service, provided the social worker maintains regular contact with the home help. The social worker maintains responsibility for the handling of the case, provided he continues to get a flow of accurate information from the home help. Even Emily Francombe appears willing to allow a certain level of what she regards as 'intrusive' behaviour, provided she feels she knows the key individual well and believes that her visitors are there to help her to live the kind of life that she wants to live. Through this 'bargain', she continues to maintain a measure of control and, possibly, self-respect.

Whereas, at the beginning, all the key actors are relatively isolated from one another, relationships have by the end of our account become much more organised. Emily Francombe has regular contact with a home help who is supported both by her own supervisor and by a social work consultant. The consultant is in regular contact with both the housing association representative and the neighbours and both of these see the home help regularly. In fact, the neighbours generally speak to the home help at least once a week. But it is not just the level of 'connectedness' or 'density' of network ties which is important but the way in which the particular pattern of connectedness organises the network and helps to ensure that support is available in appropriate ways from appropriate people at appropriate times.

Brokering care communities

A care management partnership is a good example of a 'task community'. But if those who are involved in caring for someone are to establish themselves as a 'community', they sometimes need to meet on a face-to-face basis. This is particularly so when the stresses and strains of caring lead those involved to feel frustrated and angry with one another and to search for someone to blame. All this projection of bad feelings around the network is a sure sign that the support system has become overloaded with anxiety and that its members need to be helped to come together not only to make new plans but to enable individual members to feel part of a collective effort – a 'care community' which will look after all its members and not only the service user.

This is the process of network conferencing. It has for some time been recognised that network conferences are an important care management tool (Steinberg and Carter, 1984, p.23). However, they should not only be seen as a way of working with the informal network to enhance self-sufficiency. In an earlier work, I described conferencing as 'a way of structuring time and structuring relationships in order to enable the network system to move out of a position of crisis' (Trevillion, 1988, p.302). This can be illustrated by looking now in more detail at one of the cases referred to then.

Jean Jackson was a 75-year-old woman cared for by her niece, a home help, her general practitioner and the staff of a psychogeriatric day centre. For some time this network was able to care adequately for her without any outside intervention. But I became involved after a series of increasingly anxious telephone calls which make it clear that members of the support network felt unable to cope with what they perceived to be a rapidly deteriorating situation. This message was couched in terms of a request for an assessment under the terms of the Mental Health Act.

The consultant psychiatrist confirmed that Jean Jackson was suffering from Alzheimer's Disease but could not confirm that her mental state was deteriorating rapidly, so an emergency admission to hospital appeared to be inappropriate. A network conference was called to which all the carers and a number of managers were invited, with the purpose of assessing the nature of the perceived crisis. Although there was considerable initial opposition to this strategy from some members of the network who felt that we should be acting rather than 'wasting time' talking, anxiety levels begin to drop almost as soon as a network conference was scheduled. So much so, that the conference itself was almost an anti-climax.

When we met, it became apparent that all the carers, both professional and non-professional felt rather isolated from one another. An opportunity to meet helped them to begin sharing with each other and with the social worker some of their frustrations and anxieties. The situation was no longer perceived as a crisis but as a long-term problem and from then on the way the case was handled reflected this.

Network conferencing demonstrates how the dynamics of the 'social support system' are as much a part of the 'care package' as the separate services. This particular conference began to build new mutual support mechanisms where before there had been none. It also began to clarify the boundaries of responsibility for every member of the conference so that caring became a more manageable and less personally oppressive activity. Perhaps most importantly, conferencing the problem, rather than admitting Jean Jackson to a psychiatric ward, counteracted the sense of personal failure felt by all those concerned and substituted for it a sense of collective strength.

If we look at this as an example of the brokering of a care community, it is possible to see that the way the level of 'connectedness' is developed and even the promise or hope of more 'connectedness' exercise a profound influence on the course of events. By promoting the ideas of mutual support and collective identity and responsibility, the social worker was able to reduce anxieties to manageable levels.

But even a 'task community' should incorporate opportunities for empowerment, and managing power relationships in a conference setting can be hazardous. While conferences can promote participation, it is not always possible to involve service users in them. Jean Jackson was not directly involved in the conference process herself and this decision could certainly be defended on the grounds that, for someone with severe Alzheimer's Disease or any other form of senile dementia, what may be intended as an empowering experience could simply be disorienting and frightening. However, more thought could perhaps have been given to the possibility of a two-stage process in which Jean Jackson could have met a small sub-group of people known to her and able to reassure her.

All the challenges associated with building communities in the modern age are present in the microcosm of the care management system. In particular, care managers are constantly faced with the need to find ways of enabling linkages to grow between individuals and groups who may find it very difficult to communicate, let alone develop a sense of shared purpose or collective identity. And yet, in spite of the problems, the success or failure of care management can often be gauged by the extent to which all those involved in the care management system are willing to recognise the importance of their relationships with one another and prepared to submerge differences, at least temporarily, for the benefit of all and in particular the service user.

Acknowledging this is to recognise that the brokering of social support involves brokering communities.

Brokering flexibility and informality

The intrinsic flexibility of the network conference process can lead to some very unorthodox developments. In one case, I recall a network conference taking place in the bedroom of a young woman whose combination of mental and physical problems confined her to bed much of the time. However, the role of the social support broker in generating flexibility and informality is not confined to the choice of location for network conferences.

The brokering of social support is dependent on the context in which it is practised. Moreover, effective care management depends upon an ability to be responsive to the demands of a situation rather than to impose a fixed formula of care upon it. Therefore it is probably best to see care management as embracing a continuum of caring partnerships rather than seeing it as a single activity. At one end of the care management continuum are those situations where the informal network is in difficulty but might, with advice, information and support from a case manager, be able to cope. But even here the relationships between those involved and their feelings about themselves and what they are doing may need to be explored as well. People may not want or need formal services, but they may feel overwhelmed with anxiety and/or feelings of guilt that they are not doing more. A real service can be performed simply by listening to carers and confirming that there is nothing more that they can do.

There are many examples of 'interwoven' networks consisting of 'informal' and 'formal' components where the aim is to enhance informal structures. An example might be the family of a young woman with learning difficulties and severe behavioural problems. Although the young woman cannot be left alone, the family may be able to continue caring for her with regular respite care and night 'sitters' coordinated by the care manager. An informal and flexible style on the part of the worker is particularly important when trying to build or hold together an 'interwoven' network.

But at root the brokering of social support is about informality because it is concerned with the 'quality of life'. Although it is usually argued that care management should be concerned only with specific care problems, even the most restricted definitions of care management have to make reference to the part played by the 'structure of living' or largely self-sustaining patterns of informal network support embedded in everyday social interactions (Bayley, 1973, p.316). For those seeking to broker social support more explicitly, the need to get alongside service users, in what one could call 'life-style' decisions, is even more obvious and this cannot be done except in an informal manner. Day has suggested a way forward for this type of work, based on the idea of networking 'opportunities'. He has suggested that different kinds of support network provide different kinds of 'opportunities' and, in relation to a study of people with learning difficulties, has divided these into a 'segregated' type and a type of network that allows the handicapped person access to the 'non-handicapped world' (Day, 1988, p.277). The implication of this is that all those involved in 'normalisation' work are to some extent involved in care management and that residential workers as well as fieldworkers could therefore lay claim to a role in this.

Decisions taken in this way can involve risk taking. The quality of life paradigm in general and the location of service planning and provision within a concept of brokering social support inevitably leads to some risks being taken in pursuit of 'quality of life' objectives. Service users may feel that some risks may be worth running if they improve the quality of life! However, this cannot be taken as an invitation for those employed as care managers to abdicate their responsibilities. Rather, what is needed is for lifestyle benefits to be weighed against risks and for decisions to be made in an informed way, preferably with the participation of all the members of the 'task community' that brokers will have helped to create.

It could be argued that there is still a risk that informality may lead care managers to be irresponsible in relation to their own organisations, if not towards their clients. But if the accountability of care managers is located within the broader framework of 'stakeholder networks' and inter-agency agreements of the kind which were described in the previous chapter, it should be clear that informality and flexibility can be compatible with broader roles and responsibilities. It may even be that attending to broader responsibilities implies high levels of flexibility because it implies high levels of responsiveness.

Brokering information

A care management system is a communication system. In an ideal world, the appropriate kind of information is transmitted from care managers to service providers, from one service provider to another and from service users to both service providers and care managers. But for this to work there needs to be a shared set of understandings enabling confidentiality to be respected at the same time as those involved are open and frank with one another and able to communicate in a language which all can understand. Anyone with practice experience in this area will recognise how demanding these apparently straightforward criteria really are. One way of looking at the problem of communication in care management systems is to draw a comparison with the world of computers.

Frequently we find that different parts of the same organisation have invested in very different kinds of computing systems. So long as there is very little need for the different parts of the organisation to communicate with one another, this incompatibility may not matter. In particular, if the organisation is organised on bureaucratic and hierarchical principles, all communication will be controlled by those at the apex of a number of quite distinct organisational pyramids. But if the organisational structure and culture changes, and suddenly all kinds of people throughout the organisation need to send data backwards and forwards, the problem of incompatibility becomes a major organisational headache. This is when organisations call upon the services of specialists, who set up new computer networks by making it possible for previously incompatible systems to 'speak' to one another.

This is exactly the problem faced by those organisations and professions seeking to come together in new social support systems. In order to establish an appropriate set of communication possibilities, the links between the different parts of the system need to be 're-engineered'. Here the computing metaphor ends. Computer hardware will not solve problems based on misconceptions, lack of trust or straightforward unfamiliarity. It is often relationships which need to be rethought and re-engineered, rather than technical systems. Also it is important to recognise that, unlike computers, human interaction needs to be constantly networked if it is to facilitate the kind of communication needed for effective care management. In particular, constant attention needs to be given to boundary issues so that core differences are respected and different strengths preserved while avoiding the need for defensive posturing and obstructive rivalries.

Interpersonal communication is a series of information exchanges between individuals. The social support network is therefore an exchange system in which information is passed from one person to another in the expectation that all those who give information will also receive it. The most effective care management systems are frequently those which benefit from a 'virtuous circle' in which the quality of mutual understanding improves over time as a direct consequence of the process of exchanging information and where mutually satisfying information exchanges generate ever deeper levels of trust, mutual confidence and mutual support. In other words, people are more likely to listen to one another in the future if they feel that information has not been kept from them in the past. Communication, in this way, feeds back directly into the process of developing and sustaining task communities.

Brokering care management action sets

Like orthodox care management, the brokering of social support is primarily a mobilisation strategy and the networks it helps to create and maintain are primarily 'action sets'. Sometimes people act as if care management consisted of simply asking people to deliver a particular service or, if necessary, persuading them to do so. But the process is often concerned less with persuading people to do things than with persuading them to do them together. An example dating from 1982, when I was the social worker, may help to illustrate this.

Anna Winkler, an 85-year-old woman of central European origins, lives alone in a flat which is badly in need of major repairs. She lived with a female friend for many years. Since her friend died, she has become depressed and withdrawn. She ventures out less and less and, by the time a social worker becomes involved, her increasing frailty is beginning to make it very difficult for her to continue living on her own. She is initially reluctant to have a home help or to see anyone other than the social worker. At first, it appears she is totally isolated, but, although she is alienated from her family and has few friends, it becomes clear that certain other people are interested in her welfare.

For some years she has had intermittent contact with a small voluntary organisation and someone from this organisation is very willing to be involved in the future. Likewise, her general practitioner is concerned about her and keen to help as much as he can. Someone who works in the garage opposite her flat buys her a newspaper a couple of times a week and, like the others, is interested in her future welfare. The problem here is therefore not mobilising support. That seems to be surprisingly easy. As the case develops, it becomes clear that the problem is persuading these potential helpers to coordinate their efforts.

A network conference takes place. Although the mechanic does not attend, the meeting is able to do some useful work. However, conflicts of opinion emerge almost as soon as the meeting begins and there is a possibility that no consensus will be reached and no plans made. In the event a plan does emerge. The mechanic (contacted outside the conference) agrees to ensure that he sees Anna Winkler whenever he delivers the daily newspaper and to contact the social worker if she does not appear when he knocks. The general practitioner and the welfare worker from the voluntary agency agree to continue to visit once a month but on a new pattern, so that she will see one of them at least once every two weeks. The social worker arranges to visit every two weeks but never on the same week as either the general practitioner or the welfare worker. In this way the partnership is able to develop an initial set of services which consist of a daily 'early warning' system and weekly contact with everyone else.

As time passes, it becomes possible to introduce new services, such as a district nurse and a home help and, after patient negotiation with Anna Winkler, to arrange for her to attend a day centre on a weekly basis. But new services are only introduced at a pace which is determined by Anna Winkler herself and in ways which fit in with the existing 'package'.

How was the problem of internal conflict solved? The deadlock was broken by the realisation that the key to making progress was to recognise that those present were unwilling to sacrifice their individual opinions and individual autonomy and that, to enable them to think more collectively, it was necessary to persuade them to feel that, by giving up some of their autonomy and therefore some of their (theoretical) individual power, they were gaining some (actual) collective power.

Community brokerage and care management

The model which has been outlined in this chapter can be seen as an alternative to care management or it can be seen as an attempt to return to the basic principles of linking and coordination which may have been lost sight of in the development of the 'mixed economy of care'. Much of what has been described is already present in care managers' practices in an implicit form, but a conscious shift towards 'quality of life' considerations, combined with a systematic adoption of brokerage principles, might help to restore morale and help to show that the process of organising social support need not be just a cover for cutting costs and reducing services.

7 Working together for empowerment

> Oppression often involves disregarding the rights of an individual or group and is thus the denial of citizenship. (Thompson, 1993, p.31)

This chapter is about the contribution that networking by professionals can make to the processes by which oppressed people can increase their 'involvement' in society and thereby reclaim their status as 'citizens' (Beresford and Croft, 1993). The aim is to show how social workers, nurses, community workers and others can help to dismantle barriers to citizenship through practical network activity. Networking is not the only, or even the most important, way in which these barriers can be dismantled, but professionals can apply some of the network principles that oppressed people have themselves discovered to their own work so as to maximise the potential for empowerment even in the most unpromising of situations.

The chapter looks first at self-organised or self-help networks based on a 'community of interest' and then moves on to consider the implications for professional social welfare workers.

Networking and communities of interest

The term 'community of interest' can be used to describe a wide range of 'networks of relationships' and the 'allegiances' associated with them (Barclay, 1982, pp.xiii–xviii). But here it will be used in a more restricted sense to mean a social network which develops around an awareness of oppression. It should not be confused with either the formal community organisations which are the focus of much of the community development literature or those 'communities' which benefit from the work of such organisations (Wiewel and Gills, 1995).

Networks of this kind are not mutually exclusive. They are constructed on the basis of particular aspects of social identity which are neither natural nor immutable. 'So any group of people with shared concerns/ideas/experiences are a community and we are all part of several communities at the same time' (Macfarlane and Laville, 1992, p.22). As new issues or needs are discovered, so too new 'communities' arise and, however well organised they may later become, many of these 'communities' emerge first of all as relatively informal networks; for example, it has been argued that the 'typical community-based AIDS service organisation was a voluntary, not-for-profit, non-sectarian, free-standing organisation that started as a support group' (Alperin and Richie, 1989, p.166).

Often the spur to network formation is a strong sense of a need to join others to resist some specific act of oppression. The 'web of women' created, sustained and mobilised at Greenham Common cruise missile base in the 1980s as an act of collective resistance to what was perceived as patriarchal warmongering and nuclear genocide is a good example of this. The image of the web was the symbol of the Greenham Common Peace Women. It was also the symbol of the national and international feminist network of sympathisers and activists which sustained the Peace Camp and which enabled a relatively small and often quite vulnerable group of 'campers' to be transformed at times into a massive demonstration by women capable of encircling the base.

Although it is the campaigning potential of networks like this which is their most obviously 'empowering' feature, this campaigning potential rests upon a number of other, less obvious, network characteristics. Dalrymple and Burke's 'first level' of empowerment is the 'level of feeling' (Dalrymple and Burke, 1995, p.51). If it is true that any community of interest has to reach this level before it can develop any further, the most fundamental aspect of empowerment is the sense of solidarity which can be created by linking up with others. Empowerment is therefore intimately related to what have been called 'lateral relations' (Foucault, 1979, p.238). This principle was established many years ago by pioneering feminists, but it has only more recently been explicitly connected with network development (Dominelli, 1990, p.47).

But empowerment is not only a question of feeling better about oneself. As the example of Greenham Common shows, communities of interest mediate between the personal and the political. Another example of this comes from the history of the social movement of disabled people. The social model of disability – a new and challenging way of thinking about disabled identity in relation to discrimination and disadvantage – was developed by disabled people alongside campaigns for disability rights (Barnes and Mercer, 1995).

Networking within and between communities of interest is an important topic in its own right; but for professional social welfare workers, the question is: to what extent can those aspects of empowerment which are related to patterns of linkage between individuals and groups be translated into their own work, especially as the kind of 'partnerships' with which professionals are involved are, in many ways, quite different from 'communities of interest'?

Community empowerment and community partnership

To some extent, all communities could be said to be 'partnerships', in that they all contain some element of diversity. But where this diversity includes linkages between professional social welfare organisations and oppressed people, the 'partnership' will always retain some important internal boundaries which cannot be dissolved by reference to 'common interests' and which will remain, however successfully individuals and groups work together.

It is important not to lose sight of the significance of the lay/professional boundary even where professional involvement appears to be minimal or purely facilitative, as in the case of some forms of otherwise 'autonomous' self-help (Adams, 1990, pp.26–36). This makes for a problematic relationship between partnership and empowerment which reveals itself even in the arena of community development which has always been closely associated with participation and empowerment. While it has been pointed out that professionals can help by 'building groups and networks to promote long-term solutions to people's powerlessness' (Edwards, 1988, p.39), it has also been argued that partnership can be 'disempowering for communities and especially for the most disadvantaged and socially excluded groups within communities' (Mayo, 1997, p.3).

This shows that the problems of partnership cannot be blamed entirely on the fact that 'practice skills are insufficiently developed' (Marsh and Fisher, 1992, p.9); for example, it is not always easy to tell if some of the ambitious attempts to develop 'partnerships in regeneration' now being pioneered in areas like Deptford in South London (Centre for Urban and Community Research, 1997, p.64) actually succeed in reaching out to the most oppressed sections of those communities, or whether they collude with existing power structures. At a time when people are looking towards 'partnership' as a miracle cure for urban problems, as reflected in the development of Health Action Zones, it is worth reminding ourselves that, at its worst, it may amount to a takeover of local communities by business interests (*Guardian*, 5 May 1998).

What is clear, however, is that questions of empowerment have to be integral to debates about partnership, rather than constituting a rather apologetic afterthought. Although there has been a widespread recognition of the need to involve carers and service users in planning appropriate training for those who need to find ways of 'working together' (DOH, 1993, s.2.10), it has rarely been acknowledged that collaboration itself has to be based on a collectively owned and controlled vision of social welfare (Beresford and Trevillion, 1995). One of the most important implications of this is that it involves moving away from generalised ideas about 'partnership' which can be open to abuse and which, in any case, tend to be used far too loosely to be of value, and towards a model of the 'collaborative network'.

As part of a large workshop, The West London Project asked a group of health and social care practitioners to explore the idea of collaboration in relation to specific patterns or sets of linkages running between service users, carers and a range of different professionals. Their responses showed that they wanted to see networks of this kind as lying at the centre of the whole community care process. In particular, they stressed that a greater sense of 'collective ownership' of assessment and planning brings with it a more informed awareness of the different perspectives of network participants and that this in turn helps to generate a sense of empowerment.

They were also careful to point out that, far from leading to a loss of confidence or professional identity, it was much easier to empower others if one felt empowered oneself. Empowerment was seen not as a separate skill or activity but as intimately associated with certain patterns of communication and a flexible approach to problem solving. The group then went on to specifically link empowerment to the process of exploring options for change through networks in which service users and carers were full participants.

The key issues in relation to empowerment seem to lie at the interface between interpersonal issues and community issues. Networking has been described as placing 'a particular value on inter-personal relationships and informal networks as crucial elements of a community's capacity to involve people in decision-making and to take collective action' (Gilchrist, 1997, p.100).

Some follow-up research on an anti-racist festival in Bristol involving a number of different groups discovered that informal one-to-one relationships had effectively 'underpinned the organisation with credibility, accountability and mutual understanding which continues to operate within and across more formal structures, even though the Anti-Racist alliance itself has ceased to exist' (ibid., p.103). The strength of these relationships was based on trust, respect and reciprocity (ibid., pp.104–7) which confirms that the interpersonal issues introduced in Chapter 2 of the present volume are as important for community participation and empowerment as for any other type of networking.

But interpersonal relationships have themselves to be constructed in an empowering manner. Links should be chosen by people themselves and not imposed on them by professionals.

The West London Project involved a number of service user and carer groups in discussions about community care. However, one of the groups did not fit into any of the standard categories. Asian women only agreed to participate if they could do so on their own terms. They refused to categorise themselves as 'service users' or 'carers' and wanted to be seen as women belonging to a particular community who both gave and received help. They saw what they had in common as more important than what separated them. Having an opportunity to link up with one another and thereby obtain a 'voice' in the project was recognised by them as an empowering experience, but they made it clear that, had they been forced to divide into 'service users' and 'carers' like the predominantly white groups, the whole experience would have been oppressive.

In this particular collaborative network, the component units were groups representing particular views and interests. But although the collaboration was formally one between groups rather than individuals, if the individuals in any of these groups had felt unhappy with the way in which the groups were defined then the basis of the collaboration would have been compromised. This experience appears to confirm a fundamental principle about empowerment, which is that people need to feel that the specificity of their own experience has been acknowledged in the way that they link up with others.

Service brokerage and advocacy

Within the social welfare field and away from the area of community development, the empowerment issue that has attracted most attention is the way service systems tend to reinforce professional power at the expense of those who use services, and there is no doubt that many service users feel that the way social workers and other professionals behave can make it more, rather than less, difficult for people to feel in control of their lives. 'Service users have not on the whole experienced their relationships with social workers as empowering. We have tended to view social workers as controlling, pathologising, victim-blaming, out of touch with our lives' (Wallcraft, 1996, p.39).

This is a structural problem which some have seen as requiring a different kind of approach to the basis on which services are organised and delivered. Unfortunately, little attention has been paid by these theorists to the way in which empowerment might be connected with network patterns and processes.

Service brokerage is a model of collaboration in which a professional is employed by a service user to act as a consultant and to purchase services on their behalf. It has some features in common with conventional UK patterns of care management, including the emphasis on purchasing services, but its proponents argue strongly that 'the fundamental advantage of service brokerage lies in the de-clientising of systems' (Brandon, T., 1995, pp.9–10). What seems to be meant by this is the liberating effect of having services paid for and controlled by those acting for service users.

The claims of service brokerage to be an empowering practice rest mainly on the extent to which it can transform the balance of power between professionals and service users. We do not have enough practical experience of service brokerage in the UK to draw firm conclusions about this. In the absence of firm evidence either way, all that can be said at this stage is that the proponents of service brokerage may be underestimating the power that can lie in knowledge and expertise even when it is not connected with a cash nexus. But an even more serious shortcoming may be the lack of attention given to wider patterns of relationship. If services are organised on a strictly contractual basis and managed on behalf of the service user by the service broker, it is not clear how relations between individual service providers and service users will be affected. Certainly, there seems little reason to believe that attempts to build a network on a set of strictly market principles will develop collaborative relationships, and without such a pattern of linkages it is not clear how securely empowerment can be embedded in the service system.

Another approach to empowerment which has been developed is associated with the idea of advocacy. While 'citizen advocacy', 'peer advocacy' and 'collective advocacy' tend to exclude professionals (Brandon *et al.*, 1995), there are examples of social workers and community workers working with networks of service users in order to promote these forms of advocacy (Croft and Beresford, 1990). Without disagreeing that there is a place for those employed as social workers or care managers to get involved in this kind of work (Brandon, D., 1995) or with the principle that advocacy is a useful and empowering activity, it is still possible to question the extent to which it changes the fundamental characteristics of the service delivery system. If the services which are obtained by advocates are delivered in conventional ways, it is hard to see how the overall service network could be described as 'collaborative'.

'Inclusiveness' and 'social education' as networking strategies

It may be helpful to explore briefly the issue of empowerment in a broader European context. This shows that it is possible to develop approaches which are more consistent with the idea of linking empowerment to patterns of linkage than those represented by service brokerage or advocacy and which do not require major changes in patterns of funding. The Swedish Project showed that networking strategies based on 'inclusiveness' and 'social education' can be undertaken as part of normal professional practice by hospital-based social workers.

These *kurators* saw 'inclusiveness' as closely linked to 'normalisation' which in their case took the form of a strong opposition to specialised services which might actively prevent those with HIV from using services normally available to other Swedish citizens: 'You shouldn't have to travel from one side of the city to another, you should be able to use the school that is closest so that they [the children] can play with their friends'.

Even if specialised services were being offered by a voluntary organisation or self-help group, these social workers would have been against them, on principle, if they had the effect of marginalising or stigmatising their clients. They preferred to enable people to use mainstream services and this was justified by reference to the wider objective of facilitating active participation in mainstream Swedish society. The project also showed that it is possible to think about these patterns of linkage in a wider framework, where empowerment is related, not only to the quality of the relationships within a particular network, but to the location of that network in society as a whole.

The Swedish *kurators* were concerned not just with the quality and orientation of linkages and relationships in the service network but also with the inclusionary or exclusionary attributes of other relationships important to service users. This meant that, if they became aware of prejudice and discrimination within the situations to which their clients were exposed, they felt that it was part of their responsibility to meet those concerned and to engage in a process of social education. Typically, this would not directly involve the service user but it would challenge discriminatory attitudes and practices and therefore do something to redress the balance of power in favour of service users, enhancing their long-term ability to participate in society: 'We often go out talking to different people ... if we feel there is discrimination and our clients are being discriminated against, we talk to groups, bosses or whatever's necessary.'

Developing collaborative linkages involves changing the relationship between service users and professionals and addressing the kind of problems which service brokerage and advocacy theorists have identified with conventional service planning and delivery systems. But it also involves attending to the patterns of linkage associated with service delivery and other social networks. It is a matter not just of attending to the quality of relationships within these networks but also of ensuring that the kind of links which people have are consistent with the broader principles of community participation.

Empowerment and community brokerage

Ensuring that 'task communities' based on collaborative networks are empowering involves solving some of the problems associated with the complexity of these 'communities'. This almost always requires some form of community brokerage. On a large scale, 'New Community Partnerships', which have been defined as 'the bringing together of a single community for joint action and the bringing together of different communities that have a shared interest in tackling local problems' (Macfarlane and Laville, 1992, p.22) appear to need a 'strong networking organisation' capable of building a community 'movement' (ibid., p.111). At the other extreme, even relatively small carers' networks may require some kind of community brokerage in the early stages of their formation and possibly in the longer term as well. This is because people may not automatically identify with one another.

Grant and Wenger suggest that, in the case of one carers' network, a certain kind of supportive connectedness, which they call 'interdependency', was needed to establish an awareness of network commonality. Working together in the same scheme for the care of elderly people led to an 'interdependency' among the helpers, frequent contact and consequent opportunities for helping one another (Grant and Wenger, 1983, pp.45–7). This suggests that the fostering of 'interdependency' may be seen as an empowering strategy in its own right, perhaps linked to the growth of what has been described as 'mutuality' (Holman, 1993, p.52) or a feeling of community.

The potential of this may not have yet been fully realised. The diaries kept by professionals involved in the West London Project indicate that, apart from references to network conferences, which are dealt with in the next section, little attempt was made to develop interdependencies. In most cases the practitioners identified a role for themselves which could be described in terms of brokerage, ensuring that a wide range of services were contacted on behalf of clients and even drawn into sometimes very sophisticated networks of service delivery. However, although this type of brokerage may have been empowering, in that it enabled service users to use a wide range of supportive services, it did not always generate the degree of 'connectedness' which is associated with a collaborative network.

Making changes

One of the tests which one might want to apply to any claim about empowerment is whether it has led to some identifiable change in the position of those who have been experiencing discrimination and disadvantage. But when we come to think of care management, the care programme approach or other small-scale aspects of social welfare activity, it may not be immediately obvious how social welfare workers principally concerned with service planning and provision can become involved with broader change processes as part of an overall commitment to empowerment.

One idea which has emerged is the possibility of breaking down some of the barriers between professionals and service users in the belief that this will have tangible benefits. Some feel that the needs of black disabled people will never be effectively met unless there is a greater involvement of black workers in care management. 'If Black workers do not have care management responsibility it may be difficult for them to design and negotiate a package of provision which challenges racism and empowers a Black Disabled person' (Begum *et al.*, 1994, p.148). Such a strategy not only connects the care manager and the service user in a different way, it also strengthens the collective position of that community.

> The needs of Black Disabled people are not particularly specialised or complex. Nevertheless to date many large scale statutory organisations have failed to address the concerns and requirements of Black Disabled people. Therefore organisations run by Black Disabled people, Black community groups and/or Disabled people may be in a better position to take a much more pro-active role in the care management process. (Ibid., p.150)

One of the problems about discussing empowerment in relation to more specific changes is that social welfare professionals usually become involved in situations which are already changing and which may often be in crisis. As some kind of change is almost inevitable, it is difficult to evaluate the effectiveness of networking simply by comparing an actual outcome with one or more possible outcomes some of which might conceivably have been even more empowering. Instead, it may be better to look at identifiable shifts in patterns and processes of decision making which can be related to shifts in the pattern of power and control. The West London Project generated a number of examples of these shifts associated with network conferences.

One of the interprofessional discussion groups felt strongly that network conferences were a particularly empowering type of networking strategy. The group associated this with the way network conferences set up modes of face-to-face communication between a wide range of participants, regardless of their status or power. In addition, one of the diaries completed by a mental health social worker, taking part in the project, focused on the way in which a planned process of after-care and 'rehabilitation' under the terms of the 1983 Mental Health Act was managed by a network conference consisting of the client himself, a community psychiatric nurse, a consultant psychiatrist, certain key relatives and the social worker who also chaired the conference. This structure allowed all those involved to contribute to the 'care plan' and led to 'collective ownership' of decisions. It was successful enough for the social worker to describe her role simply as 'facilitative'. There were times when the social worker needed to intervene directly but on the whole she was able to describe her role with the client as 'supportive'.

It could certainly be argued that some other approach might have produced a more empowering outcome, but there was a discernible shift in the pattern of power and control in favour of the client. At the least, it seems likely that the conference process was able to bind the network very effectively together so that nobody was allowed to exert control in an unaccountable way from a position which could not be scrutinised by the other participants. The continued participation of both the consultant psychiatrist and the client and their willingness to talk directly to one another on a regular basis also indicates that the conference process was seen as fair and equitable, whatever its outcome might have been.

The particular outcome of the conference process in this case was a successful transition from hospital to hostel. But even if the overall strategy had run into problems, significant changes associated with empowerment could still have been identified. From being compulsorily detained as a hospital inmate the client had moved into a new kind of relationship with those in the after-care network. He had become a partner in a process where he had a voice in the decisions which were being made, even if his was not necessarily the decisive voice. If we go back to the original connections made between citizenship and empowerment, it is hard to resist the conclusion that the conference process enhanced this man's citizenship status by locking network relationships into a collaborative modality which continued for the whole period of after-care support and supervision.

My own experience of chairing network conferences over a period of five years supports this conclusion about the empowering implications of the processes involved. The tendency towards higher and higher levels of 'connectedness' contributes to the development of a sense of 'community' among the conference members which also acts as a very effective constraint on unilateral action. However, it is important not to overstate the degree to which conference members identify with one another. A network conference is a 'task community' which may share certain aims and objectives but which is characterised by continuing and important differences between its members. The case for the empowering potential of such a conference does not rest on its ability to eradicate these differences but rather on its capacity to provide frameworks within which those differences can be acknowledged and collaboration can flourish.

A field approach to empowerment

Whether we focus on particular activities such as social education or particular processes like conferencing, this chapter has drawn attention to the relationship between empowerment and the internal and external characteristics of particular 'social fields'. In general, it has been argued that, although professional social workers or nurses rarely work with 'communities of interest', they can see the networks with which they are involved as potentially empowering and they can try to consciously influence patterns of linkage so as to share power and to create the kind of opportunities for groups and individuals which can combat discrimination and disadvantage.

8 Networking with children and families

Work with children and families has become identified with 'law and order' issues and therefore presents a challenge to any way of working based
on social network principles. But the tide may be turning. 'In all countries
of the European Community, there is an increasing recognition that it is
impossible to help children effectively without taking into account their
origins, family networks and cultural environments' (Colton and Hellinckx,
1994, p.565). In the UK, the passing of the Children Act in 1989 was associated with the introduction of the idea of 'partnership practice'. 'The Act
implies not only a degree of flexibility in how support services might be
delivered but also a different relationship between the providers of services
and their users' (Butler and Roberts, 1997, p.91). While much attention has
been given to the more formal implications of this, including a significant
shift in the legal context, the main thrust of the Act was to encourage social
workers to explore more informal ways of supporting families. It is therefore timely to consider the possible contribution of network-oriented approaches to the general support of families and, in particular, the detection,
prevention and treatment of child abuse.

Network assembly

The earliest – and in some ways still the most radical – of the network
approaches to family support was 'network assembly', a branch of family
therapy. The essential insight of network assembly was that the pattern of
relationships in a family network is like a shifting kaleidoscope which can
move from a 'malfunctioning' pattern to a more supportive one (Speck and

Attneave, 1973, p.6). Network assembly makes a number of far-reaching claims which include 'resocialisation' of the nuclear family unit within the broader family network, 'demystification' of the network and the removal of pathological network 'secrets' and 'collusions' by the power of what has been called the 'network effect' (ibid., pp.15–16). The 'network effect' is essentially a collective experience which Speck and Attneave describe in semi-mystical terms as 're-tribalisation': the rediscovery of a 'vital element of relationship and pattern that has been lost' (ibid., p.7).

There are few recorded examples of network assembly in the UK, but in the USA it has been more widely used, often in situations where the identified patient has been diagnosed as mentally ill or seriously 'disturbed' in some way and the immediate family do not feel able to cope. The explanation for its relative unpopularity in the UK probably resides in the time-consuming nature of the logistical task, the complexities involved in handling sessions involving large numbers of people and the fear of losing control of the whole process, as much as in the professional apathy noted by Ballard and Rosser (1979).

Beneath the hyperbole and romanticism of network assembly lie valuable insights about the nature of social support and the dynamics of network change. It has drawn attention to the problems which arise within isolated nuclear family units and the possibility of helping such families to relocate themselves within a 'community' of some kind. However, the assumption that support can only be found in a revival of the extended kinship network could be dangerous. What might the effect be of a network assembly on a young girl whose 'disturbed' behaviour may be an attempt to communicate the sexual abuse she had suffered within her extended family?

Family group conferences

In recent years an alternative has emerged to the focus on pathological or dysfunctional families associated with family therapy. Building on some aspects of network assembly, the family group conference approach places great store by two complementary values. The first of these is the concept of 'family competence', the belief that families can act rationally and constructively rather than simply acting out their problems. The second is the concept of 'reciprocity', the idea that families should be seen as including the extended family and other parts of the community and that the whole should constitute a gigantic exchange system (Hudson *et al.*, 1996, p.3).

One feature of this approach is the key role played by 'coordinators' who observe a strictly independent and yet pivotal position within the systems set up by the conference process (ibid., p.7). As with many other early examples of networking, the origins of this approach lay in the response of welfare agencies to the challenge of working with neglected minority groups. In this case, it was the need to find innovative ways of working with the family and clan systems of the New Zealand Maori. Placing responsibility back with families and communities was a recognition of cultural realities in New Zealand but also a product of a wish to create a new 'partnership between the State and the community' (Hassell, 1996, pp.18–19).

Family group conference coordinators have sought to 'challenge child welfare thinking that focuses on the individual failings of care givers and, as a result, can promote a communal sense of responsibility for child and family well-being' (Pennell and Burford, 1996, p.207). Because they alone make decisions about who should be present or who should be excluded from conferences, in New Zealand, at any rate, coordinators can exercise considerable power (Connolly, 1994, p.91). In spite, or perhaps because of this, it has been argued that family group conferences can be 'a concrete means of empowering families to make their own decisions and find their own solutions' (ibid., p.100).

The weaknesses of this approach are similar to those of the original network assembly school of family therapy in that the concept of 'coordination' implies a pre-existing family and community resource system which can be mobilised effectively. Also, while it is in many ways more realistic than network assembly, it is also less influenced by network or 'relational' perspectives.

None of this means that constructive use cannot be made of elements of both the network assembly and family group conference approaches. We just need to make fewer assumptions about families and communities. Work with families easily becomes entangled with the worker's assumptions about how family members should relate to one another. However, there is no need for networking strategies to be over-influenced by these normative expectations. In fact, one of the strengths of the network approach should be its flexibility. This means that networking can be used to challenge the assumptions and perspectives of the extended family network as well as to encourage it to take more responsibility.

One of the practice examples provided by the *kurators* who took part in the Swedish Project was of a meeting which could be described as a 'network assembly' or as a 'family group conference' but, in fact, did not fit easily into either of these categories. The meeting was focused on the needs of a child whose mother had just died of AIDS. The *kurator* who described it started by saying that she was only one of the participants and the idea for the meeting came from another social worker. She then went on to talk about both the process and the outcome.

She took the initiative to arrange a social network meeting where she invited the boy, the new [foster/adoptive] family, the teacher, the child psychologist, the grandfather, people from the social welfare office, and me. So we were sitting all bunched, discussing what had happened and taped it. Her idea was that the son would have something to take with him. It [the conference] had the possibility of explaining some things because they [the family] wanted to blame the Spanish man who had infected the woman. So I could really say that was not how it was. And the boy was there. That was really a nice experience. It was a good way of finishing with this family.

What is noticeable about this account is that there is no emphasis on anything like the 'retribalisation' associated with network assembly, or even any attempt to generate the kind of collective sense of responsibility associated with family group conferences. Rather, the aim seems to be to set up a situation wherein the boy can listen to a variety of different perspectives about the death of his mother and thereby counterbalance the views of his grandparents with those of others, not related to the mother, who took a much wider and less punitive view.

Even one example of this kind is enough to suggest that social networks can have therapeutic effects without these having to be associated with the aim of recreating an extended family or kinship-based 'community', and social networks can collectively support an individual in difficulty without needing always to take on specific responsibilities for problem solving. Similarly, networking relies less upon concepts of 'family' or even traditional ideas about 'community' and 'neighbourhood' than upon more flexible concepts of supportive interaction and communication. It is much less concerned with normative expectations about how people should act than with the processes of social interaction and how these can be worked with on behalf of children and those who are important to them.

The networking approach to work with children

The networking approach to work with children and families draws on much the same body of theory as that of any other kind of networking. It is concerned with the interpersonal domain and its association with personal networks, the importance of building and maintaining communities, promoting flexibility and informality, developing effective communication networks and mobilising resources to meet need. As in many other areas of networking practice, those involved in working with children and families will often take on the role of 'community broker', actively linking together and helping to integrate diverse social networks. However, the distinctive focus of their work raises specific issues which are unique to it.

In one short chapter it is not possible to do justice to all the different ways in which networking can be used to benefit children and young people in our society. I have chosen to look only at those types of work most closely associated with child protection, in the belief that this is where the case for a social network approach needs to be argued most convincingly.

Investigating child abuse

An investigation of suspected child abuse could be seen as an attempt to discover whether or not a child's personal network is an abusive field – a field of relationships in which abuse has been able to or could flourish. This is not just a question of the general level of family support, although this may tell us something about the probability of abuse (Garbarino, 1976, pp.178–85). We need to know whether there are specific risk factors present in a child's personal network, and just as important as any risk analysis is the need to know which parts of that personal network could contribute to a protective partnership alongside appropriate professionals.

Investigation can therefore be thought of in network terms as the development of a certain kind of communication network. To be effective, this has to ensure that, by one means or another, all relevant information can be made available at or through a child protection conference. One pre-conference strategy which I found useful both as a social worker and as a conference chairperson was to devote some time to ensuring that messages which might otherwise be too weak to get through to the conference because they were being transmitted from relatively powerless, marginal or unconventional sources might need to be boosted by the equivalent of a 'relay' in a telecommunications system. Individual professionals such as teachers or youth workers could be encouraged to take on this 'relay' function, or alternatively the investigating social worker could make direct contact and thereby ensure that the information reached the conference.

As a communication network like this rests on interpersonal linkages which may initially be tentative or non-existent, it will usually fall to the social worker involved to act as a broker by personally mediating between the various sub-sets. Handling this role effectively depends on establishing conditions of trust and confidence in the context of a tense and often highly suspicious and defensive atmosphere.

It has already been argued that a social network approach moves us away from standardised notions of the family. The implications of this are far-reaching. In terms of child abuse, the social network perspective does not make assumptions about the location of abuse, protection or support, as we can never know in advance where these lie; for example, in relation to the latter, there are strong suggestions that the strengths of black women and their ability to protect their own children have often been ignored by white social workers who have tended to make stereotypical assumptions about black families (Jones and Butt, 1995).

In addition to parents, teachers, members of the extended family, neighbours and fathers of school friends, even social workers may be potential abusers. In one situation in which I was involved as a social worker, it was discovered that a piano teacher was sexually abusing a number of children who went to him for lessons. In situations like this, parents may be the key members of a protective partnership and this may be so, even if the abuse has occurred within the family, as when it is revealed that a grandfather or uncle has been sexually abusing a child and the parents take action to prevent any further abuse occurring.

Because so much is unpredictable, it is vital that child protection workers retain a high degree of flexibility and open-mindedness in the way they conceptualise the nature of the abusive system. Having used interpersonal skills in an open-minded way to establish a communication network capable both of generating sufficient information and of relaying it to a central point in the decision-making process, the next step is to mobilise the child protection network.

Community protection

Making support and protection available to children is as important as the detection of abuse. More genuine security for a child can be provided in this way than by dramatic but intermittent interventions by social workers, paediatricians, the police or anyone else. It is here that networking has, perhaps, most to offer to those involved with working with children at risk of abuse. Networking encourages a preventative approach to the question of child abuse by focusing attention on the significance of a child's personal social network.

The likelihood of abuse is increased if children do not have a range of independent contacts with others who can exercise some informal surveillance and, if necessary, intervene to protect children or inform child protection agencies. The networking approach is then partly a matter of reducing abusive opportunities and partly a matter of enabling children to have people to whom they can turn if abuse does occur or if they are frightened it might occur. More frequent contact between children and protective members of their informal personal network can often help, as can regular contact with a known and trusted professional worker. Facilitating the growth of new relationships by introducing children to clubs or projects where they will make friends and meet responsible adults can also help to prevent abuse occurring.

In other situations, parents may be able to offer little protection because they are too implicated in the abuse themselves. Then the protective partnership may have to be based on other members of the extended family, neighbours or even the parents of the child's friends. But it may be possible to include in the protective partnership one of the parents, even if the other is the abuser.

Wherever possible, children themselves should be fully involved. Any changes in who they see, how often or where they see them, must fit into their own sense of who and what is significant. Failure to attend to the child's eye view can lead to the child undermining the very measures which are supposed to protect him or her. In the case of sexual abuse, if a known paedophile is the only person to take an interest in a child it will probably not be possible to prevent contact unless the child's needs are recognised and work is done with the child to develop other relationships which could meet those needs.

It is probably helpful to distinguish between a broader protective network and a specific child protection 'action set'. The latter is likely to be recruited from the former but may differ from other parts of it by being more directly involved in the conference process and in implementing conference decisions.

Network abuse

One of the most extreme examples of a destructive and oppressive network is one linked to the organised sexual exploitation of children. It has been alleged, but not proved, that some of this exploitation involves 'ritual abuse' (La Fontaine, 1994), but in all cases the abusive network may be able to create its own very powerful legitimating norms which can silence children (Furniss, 1991, pp.329–30) and militate against any of the abusers 'breaking ranks' and providing information about what is going on. Anyone involved in the abusive network who may want to 'confess' is likely to come under extreme pressure from other members of the network not to do so, in case they are in turn implicated.

There are therefore powerful mechanisms keeping an abusive network intact. Ignoring the existence of the abusive network and concentrating on an individual abuser and victim may leave this source of oppression untouched and reduce the chances of helping even known victims, let alone unknown ones, and do little to protect future victims of the network.

In this connection, it may be that networking has something to offer. Direct work with the abusive network as a whole is neither possible nor appropriate, but work with all those who have experienced abuse and their families – a network of the abused – can help to encourage children to talk about their experiences (ibid., pp.329–30). Such an approach might be seen as an attempt to establish an empowering network capable of challenging the oppressive power of the abusive network.

Another complementary approach might be to attempt to work with individual abusers to encourage them to talk about the abusive network. This would amount to an indirect network assessment. If an abuser is showing signs of wanting to cooperate, it may be possible to gain some information about how the network operates. The aim of such an indirect assessment would be, in the first instance, to discover ways of counteracting the pressures towards secrecy emanating from the network and to challenge the role the network might play in the abuser's own defensiveness and refusal to take responsibility. If abusers do tend to have weak ego strength and a consequent tendency to avoid reality (ibid., p. 34) then this can only add to the power the abusive network has over the individual abuser. A knowledge of how conventional and respectable networks maintain their own norms, communicate informally and mark their boundaries with secrets might be used to understand and ultimately counteract this power.

Networking may also play a part in the preventative work undertaken with abusers. At least two factors maintaining abusive behaviour could be connected with the relationship between the sexual abuser and his social network. Fear of losing his network of family and friends may prevent an abuser from fully accepting what he has done and in prison abusers may find that the only people willing to accept them are other abusers who collude with one another in denying the seriousness of what they have done. In prison, the segregation and persecution of 'sex offenders' of all kinds may reinforce the solidarity of these collusive networks and lead them to cling even more firmly to the idea that they are victims rather than perpetrators. Although reliable information on this subject is notoriously difficult to discover, the high levels of reoffending characteristic of convicted sex offenders (Finkelhor and Associates, 1986, pp.130–223) might be explicable in network terms.

To counteract the tendency for sexual abusers to form isolated and collusive networks, an analysis of how these networks could be normalised through desegregation in the prison system would be beneficial both to 'sex offenders' and to society as a whole. Although a much more thorough study of this question is needed before specific networking strategies could be recommended, work with other inmates and prison officers on the role 'sex offender' mythology has in maintaining defensive macho norms in the rest of prison could be enlightening.

In relation to abusive networks, networking is the mirror image of its usual self. The aim is to loosen ties rather than strengthen them. However, this sort of work needs to go hand-in-hand with the building of empowering networks for those who have been abused themselves or directly affected by abuse. There is a need to encourage the development of new social networks, either in prison or out of it, which could enable 'sex offenders' to help one another to resist their own inclinations and, perhaps, pressure from others to once more get involved in sexual abuse, either as individuals or as members of a network. There is also a need for professionals to stay in closer contact with 'sex offenders' on their release from prison than is often the case, to offer a mix of practical advice and support and to monitor their behaviour. These strategies would help to build a preventative community partnership.

The professional network

Certain groups of professionals are invariably involved in child protection issues. The police, paediatricians, social workers, health visitors, teachers and others form a professional child protection network. There is a need to work closely together and yet the high anxiety levels associated with this type of work can make it very difficult to foster trust and cooperation (Furniss, 1991, pp.59–113). In particular, the combination of interprofessional and inter-agency partnership and the requirement to work closely with parents creates a very challenging environment for effective decision making (Iwaniec, 1995, p.120).

All too often, conflicts which might be manageable in another context prove to be unmanageable in relation to child protection. For example, the breakdown in the relationship between the police and the local authority in Cleveland seems to have been a major factor in the collapse of public confidence in child protection services in that county. There have been numerous occasions when, as a key worker in a child abuse case, I found myself in conflict with other social workers, health visitors or teachers. The lesson I continually learnt as a practising social worker was that collaboration in such a controversial and painful area of decision making as child abuse does not work unless the ground has been prepared by some form of inter-agency work. Sometimes the results of even the most elementary liaison activities can be dramatic.

When I was working as a social worker in South London in the 1980s, the head teacher of a local primary school began to exasperate my colleagues by her tendency to overreact to indications of possible child abuse. Numerous, inappropriate conferences were called which not only wasted valuable professional time but also damaged the confidence of parents in education, health and social services. A regular meeting between a social work team manager and the head teacher was able to resolve this problem very quickly. It transpired that opportunities for an explicit discussion about the range of services provided by the local authority, combined with the implicit emotional support provided by regular meetings and the possibility this opened up of discussing concerns about individual children at an early stage, quickly reduced the flow of inappropriate conferences to zero.

However, not all conflicts between organisations are irrational. Scott has suggested that inter-agency disputes often centre on practical resource questions, preferred legal options and 'domain disputes' or arguments about who should be responsible (Scott, 1997, pp.77–9). Liaison by itself may not be able to prevent such conflicts occurring from time to time, but it will generate the kind of trust and credibility which enable conflicts to be resolved.

Conferencing

Inter-agency networking may pave the way to better mutual understanding between professionals, but there is also a need for the orchestration of child protection services around the needs of particular children in the conference setting itself. To this end, it may be helpful to think of a child protection conference as a network conference with the chair as a broker who has a responsibility for facilitating service planning as well as decision making.

Child protection conferences can be seen as a vehicle for involving parents and other people who might be important to the child in the process of decision making. As far as parents are concerned, inviting them to attend conferences and to participate in service planning creates opportunities for negotiating the part they will be expected to play. Both my own experience as a social worker in the early 1980s who helped to establish parental involvement as a norm and the more recent research on this subject (Marsh and Fisher, 1992, p.27) seem to point in the same direction. Parental attendance at child protection conferences and subsequent planning meetings can be a significant form of parental participation. It may also lead to better decisions even if it promotes conflict and dissension, as recent research about child protection suggests that consensus does not necessarily lead to good decisions (Kelly and Milner, 1996) and this in turn suggests that effective teamwork is not the same as 'groupthink'.

The implication is that enabling those with less power and influence to voice their concerns may lead to less conformism but also better and less risky decision making. Therefore an emphasis on participative and empowering processes may help to ensure that conferences do not become dominated by 'groupthink'.

Parental networks

The parents of abused children often feel very alone with their problems. Fear of other people's reactions may prevent them from talking about their feelings and experiences. Various attempts have been made to facilitate the development of support networks for abusive or potentially abusive parents (Starr, 1982, pp.46–9) and in my experience family centres can perform an invaluable function by introducing these families to one another. Providing opportunities for this to happen could be seen as networking to promote the development of a community of interest among these parents.

Where parents have felt themselves to be the victims of an injustice, they have sometimes been able to use their links with each other to launch a campaign for an inquiry, as in the case of the Cleveland inquiry into sexual abuse investigations in the county. This kind of activity is an important check on professional power and should be encouraged rather than discouraged by social workers, whatever the rights and wrongs of the particular case. If there is a concern, as in Cleveland, that only one part of the case is being put then the response should be to provide opportunities for other 'communities of interest' such as incest survivors to mobilise themselves. In this way it may be possible to ensure that inquiries and subsequent reviews of policy take all points of view into account.

Networking the child protection system

So far, we have looked at some examples of the kind of networking activity which can be systematically developed in relation to child protection issues. Child abuse acts as the focal point around which all this networking activity is generated and any one worker could be in touch with a number of separate community partnerships simultaneously. Together, all these partnerships form an interdependent whole which involves a very wide range of people and helps to relocate child abuse as a community problem, rather than thinking of it simply as a family problem. In some ways the broad-based nature of this responsibility is symbolised by existence within the UK of inter-agency Area Child Protection Committees. These are intended to bring together all the key community stakeholders in a single forum. However, there appear to be real problems in generating any sense of collective 'ownership' of these committees, which tend to be dominated by those organisations most actively concerned with investigation and statutory intervention. This leads inexorably to the marginalisation of those organisations which could make the most effective contribution to debates about prevention and ways of helping the child victims of abuse (Sanders *et al.*, 1997).

'Looking after' children

The possible contribution of networking to child protection work extends beyond the 'gates' of the care system. It can, for example, play a significant part in helping children when they are not living at home but are likely to do so again, in the near future. For some time it has been clear that, when a child leaves home and enters the care system, 'insufficient attention is given to the exploration of kin and neighbourhood networks as potential sources of support' (Packman, 1986, p.203). A networking approach would try to help the child sustain these relationships and, moreover, involve those who demonstrate a commitment to the child in the process of child care planning. Future protective partnerships may depend on this kind of work.

9 Teaching and learning

Professional education

Since 1993 I have been involved in teaching networking to groups of social work and health promotion students and I have become increasingly convinced that it can help the 'caring professions' to develop new ways of thinking about social welfare and new skills to enable them to put these ideas into practice.

A new language

A few years ago I wrote of collaboration that 'we have to find a new, softer, more malleable kind of language to describe these new working relationships – a language of process rather than structure, a language of mediation and permeability rather than one of rigid boundaries and territorial defensiveness' (Trevillion, 1996c, p.67). I then went on to suggest that a new language of this kind was needed not just to describe what was already happening but also to enable welfare practitioners to participate in the process of 'constantly breaking down and re-inventing welfare in collaboration with service users, carers and other professionals in an unpredictable post-welfare state world' (ibid.).

Nothing that I have seen or heard of since I wrote those words has changed my mind. If anything, the issue of language which I was then relating specifically to developments in community care has become central to developments in health, child care and urban regeneration, all of which, as we have seen, are beginning to focus on ways of thinking about links and linking which take their practitioners beyond the domain of traditional professional discourse.

New skills

It was the West London Project which helped to draw attention to the issue of language and it also led to the creation of a new skills profile. Again, although this profile was developed with specific reference to collaboration in community care (Beresford and Trevillion, 1995, pp.133–51), much of it now seems even more widely applicable, especially as it is not difficult to relate these skills to the five key characteristics of networking identified in Chapter 2:

- interpersonal skills (such as building trust),
- community-building skills (such as empowerment),
- communication skills (such as use of appropriate language),
- skills in promoting flexibility and informality (such as creativity) and
- mobilisation skills (such as coordination).

Cross-cutting these there are community assessment skills and community brokerage skills.

The project emphasised the overlapping and mutually supportive nature of these skills zones, rather than their separation from one another (ibid., pp.123–32). This is congruent with the idea that social networks are holistic entities, even though they may be described in different kinds of ways or have different aspects.

There was no evidence from the research project of any major differences in either the language or the skills needed by different professional groups, which is not to say that these skills might not need to be applied to very different kinds of social problems. In general, any differences between the educational needs of different professional groups are more obvious at basic professional, qualifying level than they are at more advanced levels. Those who think of development in terms of a process of increasing differentiation might find this surprising, but confident and experienced practitioners who are sure of their own identity and skills will always find it easier to focus on what they have in common with other professionals than those who have not yet developed a basic professional identity. This is not to argue against interprofessionalism at a qualifying level, but only to recognise that it can be a more central feature of professional education at a post-qualifying level.

Basic professional training

At this level, there will be differences between the kind of programmes required by, for example, health promoters and social workers. These should not be exaggerated, but they are real. In a sense, the educational task at this level is quite a paradoxical one, which could be summed up as developing a strong professional identity which can equip the newly qualified practitioner to operate successfully in an interprofessional world consisting of complex and shifting networks of partnership. It may be helpful to spell out the implications of this by continuing to use health promotion and social work as examples.

Health promotion

Health promotion has recently been defined as 'action and intervention to support and enhance people's health' (Katz and Peberdy, 1997, p.3). This opens up the topic to a much wider range of concerns than simply the traditional concept of health education, and in particular it focuses attention on the relationship between health promotion and the process of working together with a range of individuals and community groups. As a result, networking has come to be regarded as one of the skills which 'competent' health promoters need to acquire. 'Networking is clearly central to health promotion work across professional settings to share information, improve coordination, to gain support and feel valued' (Delaney, 1996, pp.27–8). My own experience of working with groups of health promoters has led me to focus on two key learning objectives:

- how to convey messages about health and illness through social networks and
- how to promote 'well-being' through active networking.

The first objective is straightforward enough. It focuses on the relationship between networking and the traditional health promotion task of effective communication. But the second may require some explanation. According to the World Health Organisation, health can be defined in terms of 'well-being' and 'well-being' in turn can be defined in social as well as biological terms. Helping individuals and groups to exploit opportunities to improve their quality of life has a direct impact on well-being and therefore health. This kind of work therefore focuses on ways of brokering new health-related resources and opportunities and can be specifically related to the goals of 'community participation' and 'empowerment' (Scrivin and Orme, 1996, p.12).

The content of the curriculum will reflect these concerns, but also draw on general networking theory. So, for example, inter-agency work and collaboration will be important, but the focus will be on ways of putting into practice the concept of 'healthy alliances' (Douglas, 1998) which has underpinned government policy since the publication of *Working Together for Better Health* in 1993 (DOH, 1993) and which argues that the goal of building a healthy community depends, in part, on establishing effective interprofessional and inter-agency networks (Delaney, 1996, pp.27–8).

Social work

In the UK, basic professional training in social work is governed by the regulations and requirements of the Diploma in Social Work (Dip SW). These have recently been revised but have, continuously, since their inception, been based on the notion of developing professional 'competence'. Any programme of organised professional learning which seeks to obtain validation by the professional body, the Central Council for Education and Training in Social Work (CCETSW) has to define its learning objectives in terms of the definitions of competence laid down in the Dip SW, and networking is no exception. But although the rules and requirements contain precise definitions of particular areas of knowledge, skill and values needed for professional social work, they do not contain an overarching definition of social work. In part, this reflects the recent history of UK social work, which has been one of diversification and specialisation. As social work becomes increasingly absorbed into the broader concept of social care, this identity crisis is likely to get worse. For a wide-ranging definition of the roles and tasks of the profession, it is necessary to go back to the Barclay Report, which defines social work as 'community social work':

> By this we mean formal social work which, starting from problems affecting an individual or group and the responsibilities and resources of social services departments and voluntary organisations, seeks to tap into, support, enable and underpin the local networks of formal and informal relationships which constitute our basic definition of community, and also the strengths of a client's community of interest. (Barclay, 1982, p.xvii)

Although many might reject this definition as in any way relevant to the challenges of present-day social work, it still forms a helpful basis upon which educators can build, enabling them to focus on specific areas of competence without losing sight of the whole picture of what professional development should be seeking to achieve. In particular, it focuses the attention of educators on the need for social workers to learn how to work with a wide range of different social networks in the spirit of community partnership.

Of course, there are some very specific issues to explore in the context of particular social work specialisms: for example, the interface between networking and care management or working with multidisciplinary child protection teams. It could be argued that the importance of the specialisms is such that there are as many different types of education and training in networking as there are pathways to the Dip SW. However, this does not mean that a more 'generic' type of programme is not also possible, focusing on the core issues identified in the Barclay Report and of value to child care and community care specialists alike. A general or introductory course or module in networking at Dip SW level might take as its starting point five key learning objectives which relate to a wide range of competences.

- How to undertake social work assessments of social networks?
- How to undertake social work in partnership with social networks?
- How to make social work interventions in social networks?
- How to evaluate the impact of social work interventions on social networks?
- How to network within and between organisations?

All of these, of course, connect strongly with the general networking issues explored in previous chapters, but they will also be strongly influenced by the fact that it is social workers who are involved. To reiterate, the core skills of networking are interprofessional, but the kinds of problems or issues which have to faced and the expectations of network partners will both be strongly influenced by professional roles and identities.

Ways of building basic professional competence

There is much about networking that can be learned from books. After all, this book is intended to communicate ideas to students and practitioners as well as academics. But there are limits to what can be learnt from the printed word. Learning about networking involves exploring ways of interacting with other people and this cannot be done on one's own, however good the book.

Although new technology can help people to gain access to information through a variety of different media, even the most interactive opportunities offered by internet web sites and discussion groups cannot fully take the place of three-dimensional learning methods such as sculpts, which are particularly useful for networking. While formal lectures may often be very helpful ways of introducing basic theory and key concepts, they are not a particularly effective way of helping individuals to work their way through practice dilemmas of various kinds, and this is often the only way in which practice knowledge, values and skills are really developed. Broadly speaking, I have found three methods to be effective: problem setting and solving, sculpting and network diagrams.

Problem setting and problem solving

Typically, this involves either distributing a fairly detailed case study or asking students to identify some problems in their own practice and then setting a number of tasks for them to work through. Health promotion students have used this exercise to explore problems ranging from sexual health to nutrition.

Exercise

As a health promoter, what kind of networks might you be trying to build to facilitate your work? Remember, social networks are patterns of contact and communication involving separate individuals, groups or organisations brought together around a common concern of some kind. It may be helpful to think of this in terms of the following:

- Who might be included in these networks and why?
- How will those involved work together?
- What kind of work they will do together?
- How might aims and objectives be clarified through negotiation?

Bear in mind: (a) interpersonal links and relationships, (b) community building, (c) flexibility and informality, (d) communication, and (e) mobilisation.

What kind of difficulties might arise in putting your ideas into practice? How might these difficulties be overcome?

Sculpting

I have mainly used sculpting to enable groups of students to explore the complex dynamics of social fields and the interplay between subjective (individual) perceptions and emotions and objective (holistic) issues. Sculpting works best with groups of at least ten students and can involve up to 20 students at a time. It can be used either in the context of a workshop or in a more conventional classroom situation. However, it is quite time consuming, so I would not advise attempting to use it unless at least an hour and a half is available for the exercise. What follows is a summary of a sculpting exercise used in the course of a one-day workshop with groups of social work students.

Exercise

All participants were divided into three groups and given information about a particular 'life event' (anything from a serious road accident to the birth of a child with severe learning difficulties) and asked to explore its consequences in network terms, one aspect of which involved creating a sculpt:

Group A: the informal network of family and friends (one has a card telling them that they are 'Ego').
Group B: the professional network.
Group C: consultation group observer+advisors.

The sculpting process starts with Ego organising the members of Group A into a pattern expressing the patterns of social interaction and social support as he or she perceives it, prior to the 'life event'. When the process is complete, members of the group are asked to comment on their positions and how they feel. Some usually say, at this point, that they want to change their positions, either to make their perceptions of their linkages more explicit or to modify the tableau created by Ego.

The next stage involves sculpting the impact and aftermath of the 'life event' and usually involves significant change in the overall pattern of linkages. Group A is joined by Group B, who take up positions in the sculpt in accordance with their professional roles and their pre-existing relationships to other members of Group B. All those in the new tableau are asked to comment on their positions, links and relationships and this exploratory process is coordinated by the observer+advisors who question each member of the tableau in turn. This concludes the 'assessment stage' of the sculpt.

The sculpt then moves into a series of experimental moves by the observer+advisors, perhaps assisted by a consultation group. As a result of this, a networking strategy usually emerges to which all members of the sculpt are asked to contribute. One key issue is discovering what it is that would motivate particular key individuals to change their patterns of interaction with others. Sometimes it is helpful to finish with a tableau representing the ideal outcome of the strategy in terms of new links and new patterns of 'connectedness'. But it is also important to enable the group to identify new problems or possible blocks on further development.

Network diagrams

I have used network diagrams with both health promotion and social work students, in combination with problem setting and solving and with sculpts. They can also be used as a form of 'homework' or distance learning, provided the material available to students is sufficiently rich and detailed. The main value of network diagrams lies in their capacity to focus attention on the need to analyse situations in a holistic way, taking account of the total pattern of interaction. I deliberately refrain from providing students with a lot of technical advice about ways of constructing these diagrams. They are asked, instead, to discover their own visual language. This never fails to produce striking and imaginative work.

Diagrams can be used either to simply help students to map out case material in a visual form or to give them a set of visual tools with which to analyse case material and to explore networking strategies. The major problem with the second approach is that drawing lines on a piece of paper can lead students to lose contact with reality, so they are required to justify lines on the paper through an accompanying written text which demonstrates not only *how* interaction can change, but why the individuals and groups concerned should *want* to change the way they are interacting with one another.

Specialist work

Most modern education and training in the field of social welfare moves from a general or common base of professional knowledge, values and skill to a more specialist orientation in its final stages. This process of increasing specialisation has become particularly noticeable in the case of social care and social work. In 1992, I developed a module on networking and care management which has since been available to all Dip SW students, but has mostly been taken by those specialising in community care. Over the years, it has become increasingly specialised.

While the module makes use of all the teaching methods described above, it focuses on helping students to acquire the knowledge, values and skills associated with a networking approach to care management of the kind described in Chapter 6. The structure of the module reflects this focus by setting networking in the context of a philosophy of community care associated with ideas such as normalisation, empowerment and participation and showing how care management can be approached from a network perspective. As the module has grown in popularity, it has had to move away from a small-group approach to one making increasing use of workshop sessions and exercises, but it continues to make use of care management material drawn from placement experiences and to combine this with more formal inputs on assessment and network conferences.

Postqualifying and advanced work

Networking can be undertaken at a number of levels of increasing complexity. At a postqualifying or advanced level, I have generally found interprofessional education and training to be the most appropriate setting for the development of networking skills and what has been elsewhere described as 'the culture of collaboration' (Beresford and Trevillion, 1995, pp.25–38). At this level, all the material can be drawn from practice with a focus on long-term developmental issues, and techniques which allow practitioners to record and then subsequently analyse their practice are particularly useful. Network diaries, already referred to as assessment tools, are very useful means not only of gathering information but also of making it possible for practitioners to analyse and reflect upon this information in a creative way (ibid., pp.39–66).

The role of educators or trainers in a situation like this is much more like that of a consultant or mentor than a teacher. Also, at this level, the distinction between education and training, on the one hand, and research, on the other, is blurred, because everybody is involved in a search for new understandings which can be applied to the further development of practice (ibid.).

Education and participation

Finally, the participative ethos of networking extends to the educational sphere. 'While it is important to make appropriate use of service users and carers as trainers, it is also important to recognise that they may have training needs as well' (Beresford and Trevillion, 1995, p.128). Working on a development project with users and carers made it very clear to me that ways needed to be found of offering opportunities to learn about networking to them, as well. As this kind of work develops it will, undoubtedly, give rise to new kinds of learning objectives and new kinds of teaching and learning strategies.

10 Conclusion

Chapter 1 of this book began with an analysis of the problem of complexity in social welfare, and it is to this theme that we now return. In some respects, everything that has been written here is an attempt to provide managers and practitioners with a survivor's guide to complexity. But, while recognising that a world of multiple accountabilities and multiple viewpoints is a potentially confusing or even frightening place to find oneself, an attempt has also been made to show that the spaces in between conventional welfare structures and systems can become a source of energy and creativity if one has some way of making sense of what is going on in this unfamiliar environment. To this end, the emphasis throughout has been on developing a coherent body of theory and showing how it can be used to map the contours of good practice in a range of welfare settings characterised by networks, brokers and gatekeepers, rather than ready-made systems of service delivery.

There has been no attempt to catalogue all the activities to which networking skills can be applied. Rather, the approach taken has been to explore the relationship between social network principles, networking processes and the roles and tasks associated with cross-boundary work and the development of what have been called 'task communities'. Ultimately, perhaps, networking is a state of mind rather than any one type of activity. It exists only insofar as network practitioners attend to the patterns and processes of the various social fields with which they are engaged and only for so long as they keep alive the values of choice and empowerment which must continuously inform their modes of interaction with others and their broad strategic thinking.

The first chapter introduced the social network concept and showed how it could be used as a framework to enable managers and practitioners to think about social situations in terms of issues such as boundary definition, 'connectedness', reciprocity and support. But by the end of that chapter it was already clear that orthodox network analysis was of limited value to social welfare practitioners who needed to know, not only how patterns of interdependency might be analysed, but also how to actively intervene in these patterns on the basis of a clear set of values.

In order to respond to this problem, Chapter 2 was devoted to developing a general theory of networking by showing how 'relational perspectives' could be translated into the elements of a new practice theory which encompassed the interpersonal and the community domains, the process of what could be called the *informalisation* of welfare, the opening up of communication possibilities and the mobilisation of 'action sets'. On the basis of these considerations, the role of the networker was then defined in terms of network or 'set' transformation.

But at this point it could be argued that all that had really been accomplished was to elaborate on the original hypothesis, albeit with some supporting empirical data. Practice theories need to be tested in as many ways as possible in order to ensure that they are robust enough to claim credibility as theories. So in Chapter 3 the theory was used to construct a model of assessment which included ways of establishing an assessment partnership and some techniques for gathering and analysing network information. This showed that it was not only possible to describe particular social problems in network terms but that 'raw data' could be transformed into useful information about matters such as the impact of patterns of interaction on perceptions and emotions, the relationship between 'connectedness' and community and the location of boundary problems, communication blocks and barriers to the mobilisation of network resources.

Having shown that networking principles could be used to construct a model of assessment, there was then a shift of focus back towards the more general question of role, in part because it was not possible to tackle the question of intervention before looking again at the question of role. While the diversity of networking practices made it difficult to generalise, it was suggested that networking often took the form of 'brokerage' and a particular term, 'community brokerage', was coined to describe this. The whole of Chapter 4 was devoted to the role of the community broker, with a particular emphasis on the relationship between this type of brokerage and the creation of the characteristic 'task communities' of modern social welfare.

The next part of the book sought to take the argument further by examining how networking concepts could generate models of intervention. Two fields of practice were selected for this in Chapters 5 and 6: inter-agency work and care management. In relation to inter-agency work, the intervention model was built around a concept of the collaborative network. In relation to care management, the intervention model was based on the concept of brokering social support.

Chapter 7 was concerned with the broad theme of empowerment, rather than any particular field of social welfare practice, and tried to show how it was integral to the whole range of intervention models, whereas Chapter 8 set itself the challenge of showing how networking could contribute to child protection work. Given the emphasis of this latter area of practice on formal legal and administrative intervention, this chapter could be seen as setting a particularly stringent test for the relevance of network models based on inclusion, mutual support and informality.

Chapter 9 looked at the ways in which networking could be taught and learnt, with particular reference to the professions of health promotion and social work.

Implications

Having established that it is possible to develop models of assessment and intervention based on a general theory of networking, what are the implications? The implications for practitioners have already been explored, but there are other, less obvious, implications as well. In particular, there are implications for managers, communities and policy makers which need to be, at least briefly, touched upon.

For managers, the major implication of a wholesale move towards networking principles is probably the extent to which they can find ways of transforming their organisations into what practitioners in the West London Project referred to as 'network-friendly' organisations, without feeling that they have abdicated their responsibilities or encouraged unacceptable risk taking. While the North London Project showed that organisations can fragment and lose their sense of direction, a broader analysis of network patterns and possibilities has shown that it is possible to combine networking with good management if individual creativity and initiative is contained within clear inter-agency agreements and wider stakeholder networks. It may therefore be that managers need to focus far more than in the past on developing these kinds of interlocking frameworks in order to ensure that creativity and accountability go hand-in-hand.

For communities, the implications of networking likewise involve both risks and opportunities. The risks are similar to those that face managers: a loss of democratic accountability and a set of service structures which are not easy of access and which are incomprehensible to all but a few network 'insiders'. But the answer to this problem is for all involved to work hard on creating new structures of participation and democratic control. Once again, these are likely to take the form of both wider stakeholder networks and opportunities to participate as service users and carers in the structures of decision making associated with the new networked welfare systems.

For policy makers, the major issue is likely to be the extent to which a vision of a wide-ranging social partnership could be undermined by a failure to appreciate that networking initiatives can only work in a legal and policy context which facilitates dialogue and collaborative ventures. Policies which encourage market competition and the protection of market advantage may not contribute to the creation of a 'network-friendly' environment. Likewise, policies which focus solely on risk reduction and the avoidance of 'scandal' may not sit well with those that focus on the long-term welfare of individuals and communities and the promotion of a social policy agenda based on citizenship and the concept of 'quality of life'.

Questions

This book is not intended as the final word about networking. A number of important questions still remain unanswered. Some of these relate to debates about 'effectiveness', others to debates about power and control. While it is easy to show that it is more effective for people to work with one another rather than against one another (how could it be otherwise, especially when the outcome measures are defined in collaborative terms), it is not so easy to specify how, under any particular set of conditions, one networking strategy might be more effective than another or, indeed, some other type of approach altogether.

One reason for this is the complexity of the subject matter. There is not much that can be done about this. Networking is a strategic response to complexity and there would appear to be little point in developing techniques for evaluating effectiveness which cannot be applied when the situation in question becomes complicated. Another reason may be that we do not yet understand enough about developmental processes in cross-boundary work. If we could predict how social networks move from one stage or state to another, we might be able to show how particular network interventions usher in these changes. But there may be more profound philosophical/ethical difficulties as well.

Effectiveness in this context has to be compatible with the sharing of power and control, the creation of more opportunities and therefore, almost inevitably, more unpredictability. Devising appropriate outcome measures in situations where a multiplicity of outcomes may be not only possible but desirable will not be easy. There will always be a danger of distorting the process of the work simply in order to ensure that it can be fitted into an overly rigid evaluative template. This would be an abuse of power which would be incompatible with the value system which, it has been proposed, should be integral to the networking approach. On the other hand, too loose a framework may make it impossible to say anything meaningful about what 'works' and what does not. Simplistic outcome measures are always likely to be inappropriate in relation to networking. This is not to say that more sophisticated techniques cannot be devised with networking in mind, but only that some regard needs to be had to the problems associated with complexity and participation when such techniques are being devised.

Themes of power and control have permeated this book and one chapter was devoted to the subject of empowerment. However, some uneasy questions remain which need further exploration. While it is possible to show that networking can be used to empower individuals and groups and to develop more authentic forms of partnership, there is a conundrum about power at the heart of networking for which there appear, as yet, to be few wholly satisfying answers. The conundrum is this: while networkers aim to share power and encourage maximum participation in decision making, they can succeed in these aims only insofar as they are able to exercise influence and thereby effect change. Rather than denying that there is some power associated with networking, there is a need to explore how this kind of power can not only coexist with empowerment but actually help to promote it.

Much work remains to be done, but the direction and, more important, the spirit of the enterprise is clear. Whereas theories like psychoanalysis or Marxism make sweeping claims about human nature, the laws of the mind or the laws of history, networking remains cheerfully agnostic on these matters. It requires no great leap of faith, only a stubborn belief in the ability of people to find strength, purpose and power in and through their relationships with others. While it would be foolish to pretend that all human problems can be solved by social networks, 'relational' perspectives open up a range of perhaps uniquely flexible, open-ended, supportive and empowering strategies which are well suited to the demands of our time.

Bibliography

Abrams, P. (1980), 'Social change, social networks and neighbourhood care', *Social Work Service*, 22 February, pp.12–23.

Abrams, P., Abrams, S., Humphrey, R. and Snaith, R. (1989), *Neighbourhood Care and Social Policy*, London: HMSO.

Adams, R. (1990), *Self-Help, Social Work and Empowerment*, Basingstoke: Macmillan.

Adler, S. (1987), 'Models of Care in the Hospital and the Community', in S. Williams (ed.), *Caring for People with AIDS in the Community*, report of a conference held at the Institute of Education, University of London, 25 March, London: King Edward's Hospital Fund for London, pp.11–13.

Alperin, D.E. and Richie, N.D. (1989), 'Community based AIDS service organizations: challenges and educational preparation', *Health and Social Work*, **14** (3), August, pp.165–73.

Anderson, B. (1983), *Imagined Communities: Reflections on the origin and spread of nationalism*, London: Verso.

Auslander, G.K. (1988), 'Social networks and health status of the unemployed', *Health and Social Work*, **13** (3), pp.191–200.

Auslander, G.K. and Litwin, H. (1987), 'The parameters of network intervention: a social work application', *Social Services Review*, **61** (2), June, pp.305–18.

Auslander, G.K. and Litwin, H. (1988), 'Social networks and the poor: toward effective policy and practice', *Social Work*, **33** (3), May–June, pp.234–8.

Austin, C.D. (1983), 'Case management in long-term care: options and opportunities', *Health and Social Work*, **8** (1), pp.16–30.

Baistow, K. (1995), 'Liberation and regulation: some paradoxes of empowerment', *Critical Social Policy*, 42, winter, pp.34–46.

Baker, J. (1996), 'Volunteer partners give a voice to the frail elderly', *Care Plan*, **3** (1), pp.27–9.

Bakker, B. and Karel, M. (1983), 'Self Help: Wolf or Lamb?' in D.Pancoast, P. Parker and C. Froland (eds), *Re-discovering Self-Help* , London: Sage Publications, pp.159–81.

Ballard, R. and Rosser, P. (1979), 'Social Network Assembly', in D. Brandon and B. Jordan (eds), *Creative Social Work*, Oxford: Basil Blackwell, pp.69–84.

Barclay, P.M. (1982), *Social Workers: Their role and tasks*, London: National Institute for Social Work/Bedford Square Press.

Barnes, J.A. (1954), 'Class and committees in a Norwegian island parish', *Human Relations*, 7, pp.39–58.

Barnes, J.A. (1969), 'Networks and Political Process' in J.C. Mitchell (ed.), *Social Networks in Urban Situations: Analyses of personal relationships in Central African towns*, Manchester: Manchester University Press, pp.51–76.

Barnes, J.C. and Mercer, G. (1995), 'Disability: emancipation, community participation and disabled people', in G. Craig and M. Mayo (eds), *Community Empowerment: A reader in participation and development*, London: Zed books, pp.33–45.

Bayley, M.J. (1973), *Mental Handicap and Community Care: a study of mentally handicapped people in Sheffield*, London: Routledge & Kegan Paul.

Bayley, M.J. (1978), *Community Oriented Systems of Care*, Berkhamstead: The Volunteer Centre.

Begum, N., Hill, M. and Stevens, A. (1994), *Reflections: Views of black disabled people on their lives and community care*, paper 32.3, London: CCETSW.

Bennett, R. (1980), *Ageing, Isolation and Resocialisation*, London: Van Nostrand Reinhold.

Berelson, B. (1952), *Content Analysis in Communication Research*, New York: Aldine.

Beresford, P. and Croft, S. (1986), *Whose Welfare: Private Care or Public Services?*, Brighton: Lewis Cohen Urban Studies, Brighton Polytechnic.

Beresford, P. and Croft, S. (1993), *Citizen Involvement: a practical guide for change*, Basingstoke: Macmillan.

Beresford, P. and Trevillion, S. (1995), *Developing Skills for Community Care: A collaborative approach*, Aldershot: Arena.

Bernal, M. (1991), *Black Athena: The Afroasiatic roots of classical civilization*, London: Vintage Books.

Bibbington, A. and Tarvey, K. (1996), *Needs Based Planning for Community Care: A discussion paper*, 1206/2, Canterbury: PSSRU, University of Kent.

Bibbington, A. and Warren, P. (1988), *AIDS: the local authority response*, Canterbury: PSSRU, University of Kent.

Blaikie, N. (1993), *Approaches to Social Enquiry*, Cambridge: Polity Press.

Bloom, H. (1995), 'Health Promotion in Primary Care', in Health Education Authority, (ed.), *Health Promotion in Primary Care: The way forward*, London: Health Education Authority, pp.1–6.

Bott, E. (1957), *Family and Social Network: Roles, norms and external relationships in ordinary urban families*, London: Tavistock.

Bott, E. (1971), *Family and Social Network: Roles, norms and external relationships in ordinary urban families*, 2nd edition London: Tavistock.

Brandon, D. (1995), 'Will you go into the risk business?', *Care Plan*, **2** (1), pp.12–13.

Brandon, D., Brandon, A. and Brandon, T. (1995), *Advocacy-Power to People with Disabilities*, Birmingham: Venture Press.

Brandon, T. (1995), 'Would you be a service broker?', *Care Plan*, **1** (3), pp.9–11.

British Association of Social Workers (1980), *Clients are Fellow Citizens: Report of the working party on client participation in social work*, Birmingham: BASW Publications.

Bulmer, M. (1987), *The Social Basis of Community Care*, London: Unwin Hyman.

Butler, I. and Roberts, G. (1997), *Social Work with Children and Families*, London: Jessica Kingsley.

Caplan, G. (1974), *Support Systems and Community Mental Health: Lectures on concept development*, New York: Behavioural Publications.

Centre for Urban and Community Research (1997), *City Challenge in Deptford: Deptford city challenge evaluation report – final report*, London: Goldsmiths College.

Challis, L. (1990), *Organising Public Social Services*, Harlow: Longman.

Children Act (1989), London: HMSO.

CM 849 (1989), *Caring for People: Comunity care in the next decade and beyond*, London: HMSO.

Collins, A.H. and Pancoast, D.L. (1976), *Natural Helping Networks: A Strategy*, Washington, DC: National Association of Social Workers.

Collins, J. (1989), 'Power and community care: implications of the Griffiths Report', British Association for Social Anthropology in Policy and Practice, Newsletter no. 4, p.12.

Colton, M. and Hellinckx, W. (1994), 'Residential and foster care in the European Community: Trends in policy and practice', *British Journal of Social Work*, **24** (5), pp.559–76.

Community Care (1997), 23–9 October.

Connolly, M. (1994), 'An act of empowerment: The Children, Young Persons and their Families Act (1989)', *British Journal of Social Work*, **24** (1), pp.87–100.

Cooper, A. (1989), 'Neighbourhood and Network: A model from practice', in G. Darvill and G. Smale (eds), *Partners in Empowerment: Networks of Innovation in Social Work*, London: PADE/NISW.

Cooper, A. and Pitts, J. (1989), 'Getting Back to Normality – Anti-Racism, Anti-Sexism and After', paper presented to the *Second Biennial Seminar on Theoretical Concepts and their Relationship to the Curriculum*, organised by the European Regional Group of the International Association of Schools of Social Work at Bled, Yugoslavia.

Cooper, M. (1980), 'Normanton: Interweaving Social Work and the Community', in R. Hadley and M. McGrath (eds), *Going Local: Neighbourhood Social Services*, NCVO Occasional Paper 1, London: Bedford Square Press, pp.29–40.

Cornwell, A. (1992), 'Tools for our trade? Rapid or participatory rural appraisal and anthropology', *Anthropology in Action*, 13, pp.12–14.

Croft, S. and Beresford, P. (1989), 'User-involvement, citizenship and social policy', *Critical Social Policy*, issue 26, 9 (2), pp.5–18.

Croft, S. and Beresford, P. (1990), *From Paternalism to Participation: Involving people in social services*, London: Open Services Project/Joseph Rowntree Foundation.

Croydon Strategic Projects (1997), *Anti-Poverty: Draft strategy for consultation*, Croydon: London Borough of Croydon.

Dalrymple, J. and Burke, B. (1995), *Anti-Oppressive Practice*, Buckingham: Open University Press.

Day, P.R. (1988), 'Social networks and social work practice', *Practice*, 2 (3), pp.269–84.

Delaney, F. (1996), 'Theoretical Issues in Intersectoral Collaboration', in A. Scrivin and J. Orme (eds), *Health Promotion: Professional perspectives*, Basingstoke: Macmillan/Open University, pp.22–32.

DOH (1991), *Working Together Under the Children Act (1989)*, London: HMSO.

DOH (1993), *Working Together for Better Health*, London: HMSO.

DOH/SSI (1991a), *Care Management and Assessment: Managers' guide*, London: HMSO.

DOH/SSI (1991b), *Care Management and Assessment: Summary of Practice Guidance*, London: HMSO.

Dominelli, L. (1988), *Anti-Racist Social Work*, London: Macmillan.

Dominelli, L. (1990), *Women and Community Action*, Birmingham: Venture Press.

Dominelli, L. and McLeod, E. (1989), *Feminist Social Work*, London: Macmillan.

Douglas, M. (1973), *Natural Symbols: Explorations in cosmology*, Harmondsworth: Penguin.

Douglas, R. (1998), 'A Framework for Healthy Alliances', in A. Scrivin (ed.),

Alliances in Health Promotion: Theory and practice, Basingstoke: Macmillan, pp.3–17.

Douglas, T. (1986), *Group Living: The application of group dynamics in residential settings*, London: Tavistock.

Dourado, P. (1990), 'American dreams come true', *Social Work Today*, 21 (25), pp.16–17.

Dowding, K. (1995), 'Model or metaphor? A critical review of the policy network approach', *Political Studies*, XLIII, pp.136–58.

Drennan, V. (1988), *Health Visitors and Groups: Politics and Practice*: London: Heinemann.

Dube, R. (1994), 'Brokers for care: CPNs and the care programme approach', *Mental Health Nursing*, 14 (3), pp.23–5.

Duggan, M. (1995), *Primary Health Care: A prognosis*, London: Institute for Public Policy Research.

Durkheim, E. (1933), *The Division of Labour in Society*, New York: Macmillan.

Edwards, R. (1988), 'Issues for Community Projects Developing Local Involvement', in P. Henderson (ed.), *Working with Communities*, London: The Children's Society, pp.29–43.

Eisenstadt, S.N. and Roniger, L. (1980), 'Patron–Client Relations as a Model of Structuring Social Exchange', *Comparative Studies in Society and History*, 22, pp.42–7.

Elias, N. (1978), *What is Sociology?*, London: Hutchinson.

Ellis, J. (1989), *Breaking New Ground*, London: Bedford Square Press.

Epstein, A.L. (1969), 'Gossip, Norms and Social Network' in J.C. Mitchell (ed.), *Social Networks in Urban Situations: analyses of personal relationships in Central African Towns*, Manchester: Manchester University Press, pp.117–27.

Etzioni, A. (1995), *The Spirit of Community*, London: Fontana.

Finkelhor, D. and Associates (1986), *A Sourcebook on Child Sexual Abuse*, London: Sage.

Fitzpatrick, R., Boulton, M. and Hart, G. (1989), 'Gay Men's Sexual Behaviour in Response to AIDS – insights and problems', in P. Aggleton, G. Hart and P. Davies (eds), *AIDS: Social representations, social practices*, London: The Falmer Press, pp.127–46.

Foucault, M. (1979), *Discipline and Punish: The birth of the prison*, Harmondsworth: Penguin.

Freeman, L.C., White, D.R. and Romney, A.K. (eds) (1989), *Research Methods in Social Network Analysis*, Fairfax, VA: George Mason University Press.

Froland, C., Pancoast, D.L., Chapman, N.J. and Kemboko, P.J. (1981), 'Linking Formal and Informal Support Systems', in B.H. Gottleib (ed.), *Social Network and Social Support*, London: Sage, pp.259–75.

Furniss, T. (1991), *The Multi-Professional Handbook of Child Sexual Abuse: Integrated Management, Therapy and Legal Intervention*, London: Routledge.

Gaitley, R. and Seed, P. (1989), *HIV and AIDS: A social network approach*, London: Jessica Kingsley.

Garbarino, J.G. (1976), 'Some ecological correlates of child abuse: the impact of socio-economic stress', *Child Development*, 47, pp.178–85.

Garbarino, J. (1983), 'Social Support Networks: Rx for the Helping Professions' in J.K. Whittaker and J. Garbarino (eds), *Social Support Networks: Informal Helping in the Social Services*, New York: Aldine, pp.3–28.

Garbarino, J.G. (1986), 'Where does social support fit into optimizing human development and preventing dysfunction?', *British Journal of Social Work*, 16, Supplement, pp.23–37.

Gay, P. (1983), 'Action Learning and Organisational Change', in M. Peddlar (ed.), *Action Learning in Practice*, London: Gower, pp.153–64.

Gergen, M. (1995), 'The Social Construction of Personal Histories: Gendered lives in popular autobiographies' in T.R. Sarbin and J.I. Kitsuse (eds), *Constructing the Social*, London: Sage, pp.19–44.

Gilchrist, A. (1997), 'A more excellent way: developing coalition and consensus through informal networking', *Community Development Journal*, 33 (2), pp.100–108.

Gittins, D. (1985), *The Family in Question: Changing households and familiar ideologies*, London: Macmillan.

Glaser, B.G. and Strauss, A.L. (1968), *The Discovery of Grounded Theory*, London: Weidenfeld & Nicolson.

Goffman, E. (1968), *Asylums: Essays on the social situation of mental patients and other inmates*, Harmondsworth: Penguin.

Goffman, E. (1971), *The Presentation of Self in Everyday Life*, Harmondsworth: Penguin.

Goodman, L.A. (1961), 'Snowball sampling', *Annals of Mathematical Statistics*, 32, pp.148–70.

Gostick, C. (1997), 'From Joint Commissioning to Effective Partnerships, Case Study 18', *Community Care Management and Planning Review*, 5 (6), December, pp.193–201.

Grant, G. and Wenger, C. (1983), 'Patterns of Partnership: three models of care for the elderly', in D. Pancoast, P. Parker and C. Froland (eds), *Rediscovering Self-Help*, London: Sage Publications, pp.27–51.

Greif, G.L. and Porembski, E. (1988), 'AIDS and Significant Others: findings from a preliminary exploration of needs', *Health and Social Work*, 13 (4), pp.259–65.

Griffiths, R. (1988), *Community Care: Agenda for Action*, London, HMSO.

Guardian, 5 May 1998.

Habermas, J. (1972), *Knowledge and Human Interests*, London: Heinemann.

Hadley, R. and McGrath, M. (1980), *Going Local: Neighbourhood social services*, London: Allen & Unwin.

Hadley, R., Cooper, M. and Stacy, G. (1987), *A Community Social Worker's Handbook*, London: Tavistock.

Hall, R. (1988), 'The Inter-Agency Approach', in P. Henderson (ed.), *Working With Communities*, London: The Children's Society, pp.82–92.

Hall, R.H. (1995), *Complex Organisations*, Aldershot: Dartmouth.

Hassell, I. (1996), 'Origins and Development of Family Group Conferences', in J. Hudson, A. Morris, G. Maxwell and B. Galaway (eds), *Family Group Conferences: Perspectives on policy and practice*, Annandale, Australia: The Federation Press/Criminal Justice Press, pp.17–36.

Henderson, P. (ed.) (1988), *Working With Communities*, London: The Children's Society.

Henderson, P. and Thomas, D.N. (1987), *Skills in Neighbourhood Work*, London: Allen & Unwin.

Hewitt, R. (1986), 'Community Mental Handicap Teams: Service provision and linkage strategies', in G. Grant, S. Humphreys and M. McGrath (eds), *Community Mental Handicap Teams: Theory and Practice*, BIMH Conference Series, London: British Institute of Mental Handicap.

Hicks, C. (1988), *Who Cares: looking after people at home*, London: Virago.

Hill, M. (1982) 'Professions in Community Care', in A. Walker (ed.), *Community Care: the Family the State and Social Policy*, Oxford: Basil Blackwell and Martin Robertson, pp.56–75.

Hoffman, L. (1981), *Foundations of Family Therapy: A conceptual framework for systems change*, New York: Basic Books.

Holman, B. (1983), *Resourceful Friends: Skills in Community Social Work*, London: The Children's Society.

Holman, B. (1993), *A New Deal for Welfare*, Oxford: Lion Publishing.

Hudson, J., Morris, A., Maxwell, G. and Galaway, B. (eds) (1996), *Family Group Conferences: Perspectives on policy and practice*, Annandale, Australia: The Federation Press/Criminal Justice Press.

Humphreys, S. and McGrath, M. (1986), 'Community Mental Handicap Teams: problems and possibilities', in G. Grant, S. Humphreys and M. McGrath (eds), *Community Mental Handicap Teams: Theory and Practice*, BIMH Conference Series, London: British Institute of Mental Handicap, pp.21–37.

Hunter, D.J. and Wistow, G. (1987), *Community Care in Britain: Variations on a theme*, London: King Edward's Hospital Fund for London.

Hutton, W. (1997), *The State to Come*, London: Vintage.

Iwaniec, D. (1995), *The Emotionally Abused and Neglected Child: identification, assessment and intervention*, Chichester: John Wiley and Sons.

Jones, A. and Butt, J. (1995), *Taking the Initiative: The report of a national study assessing service provision to Black children and their families*, London: NSPCC / Race Equality Unit.

Jones, R.V.H. (1992), 'Teamwork in primary care: how much do we know about it?', *Journal of Interprofessional Care*, 6 (1), pp.25–9.

Jordan, B. (1990), *Social Work in an Unjust Society*, London: Harvester Wheatsheaf.

Katz, J. and Peberdy, A. (1997), *Promoting Health: Knowledge and Practice*, Basingstoke: Macmillan/Open University.

Kelly, N. and Milner, J. (1996), 'Child protection decision-making', *Child Abuse Review*, 5 (2), pp.91–102.

Kettering, S. (1986), *Patrons, Brokers and Clients in Seventeenth Century France*, Oxford: Oxford University Press.

Kleizkowski, B.M., Elling, R.H. and Smith, D.L. (1984), *Health System Support for Primary Health Care*, Geneva: World Health Organisation.

Komito, L. (1992), 'Brokerage or Friendship? Politics and networks in Ireland', *The Economic and Social Review*, January.

La Fontaine, J. (1994), *The Extent and Nature of Organised and Ritual Abuse*, London: HMSO.

Laming, H. (1989), 'Meet the Challenge', *Community Care*, 3 August, p.3.

Lane, M. (1997), 'Community work, social work: green and postmodern', *British Journal of Social Work*, 27 (3), pp.319–41.

Laumann, E.O., Marsden, P.V. and Prensky, D. (1989), 'The Boundary Specification Problem in Network Analysis', in L.C. Freeman, D.R. White and A.K. Romney (eds), *Research Methods in Social Network Analysis*, Fairfax, VA: George Mason University Press, pp.61–87.

Lewis, J. and Glennerster, H. (1996), *Implenting the New Community Care*, Buckingham: Open University Press.

Lewis, J., Bernstock, P., Bovell, V. and Wookey, F. (1997), 'Implementing care management: issues in relation to the new community care', *British Journal of Social Work*, 27 (1), pp.5–24.

Macfarlane, R. and Laville, J.L. (1992), *Developing Community Partnerships in Europe*, London: Directory of Social Change/Calouste Gulbenkian Foundation.

Maguire, L. (1983), *Understanding Social Networks*, London: Sage Publications.

Maher, P. (ed.) (1987), *Child Abuse: the educational perspective*, Oxford: Basil Blackwell.

Marsh, P. and Fisher, M. (1992), *Good Intentions: Developing partnership in social services*, York: Joseph Rowntree Foundation.

Mayer, A.C. (1962), 'System and Network: an approach to the study of political process in Dewar', in C. Madan and G. Sarana (eds), *Indian*

Anthropology: essays in memory of D.N. Majundra, Bombay: Bombay Publishing House, pp.266–78.

Mayer, A.C. (1966), 'The Significance of Quasi-Groups in the study of Complex Societies', in M. Banton (ed.), *The Social Anthropology of Complex Societies*, ASA Monographs 4, London: Tavistock, pp.97–122.

Mayo, M. (1997), 'Partnerships for regeneration and community development: some opportunities, changes and constraints', *Critical Social Policy*, 17 (3), August, pp.3–26.

Mayo, M. and Craig, G. (1995), 'Community Participation and Empowerment: The human face of structural adjustment or tools for democratic transformation?', in G. Craig and M. Mayo (eds), *Community Empowerment: A reader in participation and development*, London: Zed books, pp.1–11.

McBrien, J. (1996), 'Commentary on case study 14', *Community Care Management and Planning*, 4 (5), October, pp.164–5.

Milardo, R.M. (1988), 'Families and Social Networks: an overview', in R.M. Milardo (ed.), *Families and Social Networks*, London: Sage Publications, pp.13–47.

Mitchell, J.C. (1969), 'The Concept and Use of Social Network', in J.C. Mitchell (ed.), *Social Networks in Urban Situations: Analyses of personal relationships in Central African towns*, Manchester: Manchester University Press, pp.1–50.

Moreno, J.L. (1978), *Who Shall Survive? Foundations of sociometry, group psychotherapy and sociodrama*, New York: Beacon House.

Morris, J. (1991), *Pride Against Prejudice – Transforming attitudes to disability*, London: Women's Press.

Morris, J. (1993), *Independent Lives: Community care and disabled people*, London: Macmillan.

National Health Service and Community Care Act (1990), London: HMSO.

Packman, J. (1986), *Who Needs Care? Social work decisions about children*, Oxford: Basil Blackwell.

Payne, M. (1986a), *Social Care in the Community*, Basingstoke: BASW/Macmillan.

Payne, M. (1986b), 'Community Connections through Voluntary Organisations: problems and issues', in G. Grant, S. Humphreys and M. McGrath (eds), *Community Mental Handicap Teams: Theory and Practice*, BIMH Conference Series, London: British Institute of Mental Handicap, pp.60–77.

Payne, M. (1993), *Linkages: Effective networking in social care*, London: Whiting and Birch.

Peck, E. and Poxton, R. (1998), 'Health Action Zones: towards a paradigm shift', *Health and Health Care*, 6 (1), February, pp.7–12.

Pennell, J. and Burford, G. (1996), 'Attending to Context: Family group decision-making in Canada', in J. Hudson, A. Morris, G. Maxwell and B. Galaway (eds), *Family Group Conferences: Perspectives on policy and practice*, Annandale, Australia: The Federation Press/Criminal Justice Press, pp.206–20.

Percy-Smith, J. and Sanderson, I. (1992), *Understanding Local Needs*, London: Institute for Public Policy Research.

Phillipson, C. (1992), 'Challenging the "Spectre of Old Age": Community care for older people in the 1990s', in N. Manning and R. Page (eds), *Social Policy Review*, 4, Canterbury: Social Policy Association, pp.111–33.

Plant, R. (1974), *Community and Ideology: An essay in applied social philosophy*, London: Routledge & Kegan Paul.

Rands, M. (1988), 'Changes in Social Networks Following Marital Separation and Divorce', in R.M. Milardo (ed.), *Families and Social Networks*, London: Sage Publications, pp. 127–46.

Reinhardt, A.M. and Quinn, P. (eds) (1973), *Family Centered Community Nursing: A socio-cultural framework*, Saint Louis: The C.V. Mosby Company.

Ritchie, P. (1994), 'Matching Needs and Resources – Manager or Broker' in R. Davidson and S. Hunter (eds), *Community Care in Practice*, London: B.T. Batsford, pp.133–41.

Robertson-Elliot, F. (1986), *The Family: Change or continuity?*, London: Macmillan.

Robson, C. (1993), *Real World Research: A resource for social scientists and practitioner–researchers*, Oxford: Blackwell.

Rodman, W.L. and Courts, D.A. (1983), *Middlemen and Brokers in Oceania*, ASA Monograph, No.9, London: Larham.

Rose, S. and Black, B. (1985), *Advocacy and Empowerment: Mental health care in the community*, London: Routledge & Kegan Paul.

Sanders, R., Jackson, S. and Thomas, N.(1997), 'Degrees of involvement: the interaction of forms of commitment in area child protection committees', *British Journal of Social Work*, 27 (6), pp.871–92.

Sarbin, T.R. and Kitsuse, J.L. (1995), 'Introduction' to T.R. Sarbin and J.L. Kitsuse, (eds), *Constructing the Social*, London: Sage Publications, pp.1–18.

Schein, E.H. (1985), *Organisational Culture and Leadership*, London: Jossey-Bass.

Schumacher, F. (1974), *Small is Beautiful*, Tonbridge Wells: Abacus.

Scott, D. (1997), 'Inter-Agency Conflict: An ethnographic study', *Child and Family Social Work*, 2 (2), pp.73–80.

Scott, J. (1992), *Social Network Analysis*, Newbury Park, CA: Sage.

Scrivin, A. and Orme, J. (eds) (1996), *Health Promotion: Professional perspectives*, Basingstoke: Macmillan/Open University.

Seebohm Committee (1968), *Report of the Committee on Local Authority and Allied Personal Social Services*, Cmnd 3703, London: HMSO.

Seed, P. (1990), *Introducing Network Analysis in Social Work*, London: Jessica Kingsley.

Seed, P. and Kaye, G. (1994), *Handbook for Assessing and Managing Care in the Community*, London: Jessica Kingsley.

Sharkey, P. (1989), 'Social networks and social service workers', *British Journal of Social Work*, **19** (5), pp.387–405.

Simic, P. (1995), 'What's in a word? From social worker to care manager', *Practice*, **7** (3), pp.5–18.

Smale, G., Tuson, G., Cooper, M., Wardle, M. and Crosbie, D. (1988), *Community Social Work: A paradigm for change*, London: NISW.

Smith, K. (1995), 'Individual needs swamped by tide of demand', *Care Plan*, **2** (1), pp.7–9.

Solomon, B.B. (1976), *Social Work in Oppressed Communities*, New York: Columbia University Press.

Speck, R.V. and Attneave, C.L. (1973), *Family Networks*, New York: Pantheon.

Sprott, W.J.H. (1958), *Human Groups*, Harmondsworth: Penguin.

Srinivas, M.N. and Beteille, A. (1964), 'Networks in Indian social structure', *Man*, **lxviv**, pp.165–71.

Starr, R.H. Jnr (1982), *Child Abuse Prediction: policy implications*, Cambridge, MA: Bollinger Publishing Company.

Statham, D. (1996), 'Challenges to Social Work Education', in S. Trevillion and P. Beresford (eds), *Meeting the Challenge: Social work education and the community care revolution*, London: National Institute for Social Work, pp.10–18.

Steinberg, R.M. and Carter, G.W. (1984), *Case Management and the Elderly*, Lexington, MA: Lexington Books.

Taylor, M., Langan, J. and Hoggett, P. (1995), *Encouraging Diversity: Voluntary and private organisations in community care*, Aldershot: Arena.

Thompson, C. (1993), *Anti-Discriminatory Practice*, London: Macmillan.

Toffler, A. (1971), *Future Shock*, London: Pan Books.

Tones, K. (1996), 'The Anatomy and Ideology of Health Promotion: Empowerment in context', in A. Scrivin and J. Orme (eds), *Health Promotion: Professional perspectives*, Basingstoke: Macmillan/Open University, pp.9–21.

Trevillion, S. (1988), 'Conferencing the Crisis: the application of network models to social work practice', *British Journal of Social Work*, **18** (3), pp.289–307.

Trevillion, S. (1988/1989), 'Griffiths and Wagner: which future for community care?', *Critical Social Policy*, **24**, winter, pp.65–73.

Trevillion, S. (1996a), 'Talking about collaboration', *Research Policy and Planning*, **14** (1), pp.96–101.

Trevillion, S. (1996b), 'Towards a comparative analysis of collaboration', *Social Work in Europe*, **3** (1), pp.11–18.

Trevillion, S. (1996c), 'Networking and Social Work Education', in S. Trevillion and P. Beresford (eds), *Meeting the Challenge: Social work education and the community care revolution*, London: National Institute for Social Work, pp.65–75.

Trevillion, S. (1996d), 'Hard choices in health care: patients' rights and public priorities', *Social Work in Europe*, **3** (1), pp.37–9.

Trevillion, S. (1997), 'The globalisation of European social work', *Social Work in Europe*, **4** (1), pp.1–9.

Trevillion, S. and Green, D. (1998), 'The Co-operation Concept in a Team of Swedish Social Workers', in I. Edgar and A. Russell (eds), *The Anthropology of Welfare*, London: Routledge, pp.97–119.

Wagner, G. (1988), *Residential Care: A Positive Choice*, Report of the Independent Review of Residential Care, London: HMSO.

Wallcraft, J. (1996), 'Empowerment and User Involvement', in S. Trevillion and P. Beresford (eds), *Meeting the Challenge: Social work education and the community care revolution*, London: National Institute for Social Work, pp.37–47.

Warren, D.I. (1981), *Helping Networks: how people cope with problems in the urban community*, Notre Dame, Indiana: University of Notre Dame Press.

Wasserman, S. and Faust, K. (1994), *Social Network Analysis: Methods and applications*, Cambridge: Cambridge University Press.

Weber, M. (1978), *Economy and Society*, London: University of California Press.

Wenger, G.C. (1994), *Support Networks of Older People: A guide for practitioners*, Centre for Social Policy and Development, Bangor: University of Wales.

Whittaker, J.K. (1986), 'Integrating Formal and Informal Care: a conceptual framework', *British Journal of Social Work*, **16**, Supplement, pp.39–62.

Wiewel, W. and Gills, D. (1995), 'Community Development, Organisational Capacity and US Urban Policy: Lessons from the Chicago experience 1983–93', in G. Craig and M. Mayo (eds), *Community Empowerment: A reader in participation and development*, London: Zed books, pp.127–39.

Wilding, P. (1992), 'The Public Sector in the 1980s', in N. Manning and R. Page (eds), *Social Policy Review*, 4, Canterbury: Social Policy Association, pp.8–25.

Wiseman, T. (1989), 'Marginalised Groups and Health Education About HIV Infection and AIDS', in P. Aggleton, G. Hart and P. Davies (eds), *AIDS: Social representations, social practices*, London: The Falmer Press, pp.211–19.

Index

action learning sets 78
action sets 49–50, 59, 68 (*see also*
   mobilisation); in care management
   117–9
action zones 2, 50; health 90–1
activist networks 4
advocacy 126–7
after-care 130–1
alliances 2–3
anthropology 11–12
anti-racist 125
Area Child Protection Committees 50,
   144
Asian women 125
assessment 53–69; field 59; model 62;
   partnership 54–61, process 59

Barclay Report 107
black disabled people 130
black residents 57
black workers 130
boundary 4; of social networks 21–4; of
   inter-agency network 90 *see also*
   divide
brokers 28–9, network 49–50, 71; of
   communities 114; of information
   116–7; networkers as 71; and
   representatives 91–2 *see also*
   community brokers, coordination,
   community gatekeepers, mediators
   and social support
bureaucracy and networking 95–6

care management 2, 13, 22, 103–19;
   philosophy 103–5; practice 104–5
care package 2, 58–9, 103–19
care system 144
carers 8; groups 9; links with 83; and
   professionals 60; and empowerment 125–32
case notes 8, 12
central figure 47
chairing of network conferences 4 *see*
   also conferencing
child abuse 137–44
children 133–44; in need 82
Children Act 133
choice 5–6; philosophy of 110
citizens 95; and empowement 131
civil society 3
clique 30, 35, 48
close-knit networks 22–7, 94
closed circuits 45–7
collaboration 9–11, 35, 145; in child
   protection 141–4; and cooperation
   12; culture of 8; problem of 87–9;
   and roles 44; skills 8
collaborative network 124–32
collective action 5; ownership 44;
   paradox of 5; strength 114
collective awareness 60–1
collective decisions 5, 95
collective identity 40–2 (see also
   identity) in care mananagement
   114

collective and individual 53–4
communication 45–8; networks 45, 137; assessment of 67, 89–90; between agencies 97–8; and care management 116–7; problems 59–60
communitarianism 2
community 4–6, 40, 22, 122–3; of agencies 95; assessment 53–4 (*see also* assessment); of care 112–3; data 64–6; empowerment 22; groups 3; of interest 22, 121–3; and kinship 136; and networking 157–8; participation 53, 125–8, 147; and task 40–2
community brokers 71–85 (*see also* brokers); and empowerment 128–9, 147; with families 137; limitations of brokerage 84
community care 2, 8–11, 82–4; system 82; diary 9
community empowerment 123–6 *see also* empowerment
community gatekeepers 55–6 (*see also* brokers); community health 46–7, 50
community mental handicap teams 98, 100
community organisations 121
community partnership and social partnership 1–3 (*see also* partnership); and child abuse 141; and social work 148; community social work 4; and care management 107
community work 5; and community health 46
complexity 15–17, 155; of roles and tasks; relationships 11; of situations 104
complex networks 4; development of 72; society as 54
child protection conference 75–6
conferencing 4, 73, 113–5; and empowerment 130–1, and child protection 142–3
conflict 41–2, 59, 61; in care management 119
connectedness 24–7, 39–40 (*see also* density); in care management 114; in organisations 94
consultation 111

cooperation 11–12; and collaboration 12
coordination 24, 49–50, 101; of families 134; of services 103–19 *see also* brokers
counselling 5
crisis 72–4; of network 111, 113
critical path 66
cross-boundary 4–6, 9, 15–17; and brokerage 71; linkages 35, 51; sets 51
culture 35 *see also* collaboration

data 7; sets 7–12
density of social networks 3, 24–7
diagrams 152
difference 5–6, 8 (*see also* boundary); respect for 5; and empowerment 131–2
directedness *see* reciprocity
disabled people 122–3
discrimination and disadvantage 122, 129, 131
divide between health and social care 87

education process in social networks 60–61, 76–8
emancipatory research 7
empowerment 5–7, 13, 42 (*see also* emancipatory research and power); and informality 44; and care management 103–19; and networking 51, 121–32; epistemology of networking 6–7
ethnography 77
European 11; Union 3
exchange 31, system 134 *see also* reciprocity
exclusionary 128

families 133–44
family competence 134
family group conference 134–6
family network 134–6
family therapy 133
feedback 60–1
flexibility 44 (*see also* informality); assessment of 66; in care management 115–6

genericism 1–4

Greenham Common 122
group discussions 7–12, 125
groupthink 143
groupwork 4, 56

health promotion 147–53
health visitors 45–6, 80–1
HIV/AIDS 9–11; planning 58; network
    39–40; support group 122; and
    families 135
holes in networks 26–7
holistic: care 103; definitions of need
    109
hospital discharge and partnership 91–2
hypotheticals 65–6

identity and social interaction 64–5
inclusiveness 127–8
informal networks 40
informality 44; and liaison 92–3
information; access to 5; gathering 61–8;
    hard and soft 61–2; and power 48;
    see also communication
inter-agency work 4, 50, 81–5; contracts
    100–1; definition of 88–9; partner-
    ship 89–91; networking 87–102;
    relationships 92–3; and child
    protection 141–4
interdependency 7, 19, 33, 129
interdisciplinary working 1
interorganisational: and
    interprofessional 96; linkages 88–9;
    network 89; space 88
interpersonal domain 37, 137; and
    brokering support 109–12; and
    communication 117; gathering
    data about 62–4; restructuring of
    37–40
interprofessional 41–2, 96, 141–2; *see
    also* inter-agency
interweaving 49; in care management
    107
isolation 113; of nuclear family 134

joint commissioning 2, 89

kinship network 134
kurators 11–12

language 145

learning disabilities and care manage-
    ment 104
liaison 50, 98–9, 142
lingua franca 77
linking 3, 11–12; and linkage 6, 10–11;
    strategic 71–2; of action sets 80; and
    empowerment 128; *see also* cross-
    boundary
loose-knit networks 24–7

management 157; of change 74; of
    negotiation process 83–4; of
    network messages 47–8 and
    networking 157–8; *see also*
    managerialism and care manage-
    ment
managerialism 105
marginalising 127
markets in social care 3; ideologies 2;
    effect on relationships 105
mediators 55; *see also* brokers
methodologies 7–12
micro and macro 53–4
mobilisation 49–50; assessment of
    potential for 68; of inter-agency
    resources 98–9; *see also* action sets
models 6–7
multidisciplinary teamwork 76–7
multiple identities 16
multiple perspectives 8, 17; and assess-
    ment 60–1
mutual (*see* reciprocity); support 43, 65–
    6

needs 2; assessing 53–4; concept of 107;
    and resources 27–8; and collabora-
    tive roles 44
negotiation 54–6, 59–60
neighbourhood 17–18; brokers 55;
    communication 45–6; networks
    144; and residential homes 57;
    social work 38–9, 81, 90
network analysis 32–6; and problem
    solving 74; *see also* social networks
network approaches to care manage-
    ment 108–9
network chains 80–1
network abuse 139–41
network assembly 133–4
network awareness 76–7

network effect 134
network diaries 62–3
network focus and field 56–9
network interpretation 77
network meeting 39–40 *see also*
    conferencing
network partnership 74–6 *see also*
    community partnership
network perspective 138
network questionnaires 63
network tracking 64
networkers 6–7 (*see also* roles); opportu-
    nities for 3–9; networking 1–13;
    definition of 3, 6; with children and
    families 133–44; and empowerment
    130; organisation 87, 95; and
    practice 35–51; skills 146 teaching
    of 145–53; theory of 1, 4–7, 12
New Zealand 135
nominalist 22
normalisation 26
North London Project 9–11

ontology of networking 6–7
open circuits 45–7
opportunities 3–9; for empowerment 114
oppression 121–3
organisations 6; in care management
    117; culture 87–90; flexibility of 66

packages of care or services 103–19
parental involvement 142–4
parental networks 143
participation 5–8, and participatory
    strategies 11, 42; *see also* partnership
partnership 2–8, 105–6 (*see also* commu-
    nity partnership and network
    partnership); and oppression 123;
    with parents 133; for protection of
    children 139; systems 81–5; pat-
    terns of interaction 17–20; and
    network communication 4, 67
personal and political 54
personal network 22–4; and children
    136–44
policy-makers 158
postqualifying work 153
post-welfare state 145
power 65 (*see also* empowerment); of
    service providers 107–8; sharing

78–9; structures 123; questions
    about 159
practice theory 35–51
problem setting and problem solving
    150
professional network 141–2
projection 112–3
purchaser/provider split 89–91

quality assurance 83
quality of life 3, 107–19

realist 22
reciprocity 6, 31, 39–40, 112; *see also*
    connectedness
reflexivity 7, 37–9, 111; of networks 79
relational 36; perspective 37, 135
relationships 114
research strategies 6–7; and practice 35–
    6, questions 36
residential accomodation 57–8
resources for care management 104;
    network 108; system 108
respect 37, 110; for difference 5
roadblocks 59–60
role 10–11; sets 11, 72; of networker 50–
    1, 71–2

sculpting 150–52
Seebohm Report 107
self-help 121
service brokerage 126–7
services 103–5; agency network 9;
    development of 83; packages of
    103–19
service users 8–9, 40, 83, 90–1; in care
    management 103–19; and empow-
    erment 124–32
sets 5–6, 21–4, 51 *see also* cross-bound-
    ary sets
sex offenders 140–41
sexual abuse 134, 143
social change 20–1; brokering of 72–6;
    legitimating 74–6; mandate for 74–
    6; promoting 67
social constructionism 7–8
social exclusion 27; and exclusionary
    networks 29–30; *see also*
    exclusionary and social
    marginalisation

social field 18–20; and empowement 130–1
social interaction 7; external 10; network 10; and assessment 61–2; and problem-solving 74
social marginalisation 27; *see also* social exclusion
social model of disability 122
social network 1, 3, 5, 11–12; 15–33; conferences 4; *see also* networks and conferencing
social solidarity 3
social services 1, 10; department 1, 8–9
social support 31; brokering of 108–19; of families 133–36; network 31, typology of 31;
social welfare 2, 4, 124; organisations 11; practice 1; *see also* welfare
social work 148–53; and social workers 1
stakeholder 35; network 74–6, 91–5
stars 22–4, 58
steps 28, 30
systems brokerage 82–4, 91–2
systems theory 5; and networking 7
Swedish Project 11–12

task community 40–2; brokering of 71–

2; in care management 112–5; in an inter-organisational context 93–5; and empowerment 128, 131; *see also* community
teaching and learning about networking 145–53
teams 9; in child protection 143; concept 11; functioning 10; identity 15–16
transmitter 47
trust 38, 50; and child protection 137; between organisations 92–3

user groups 8

virtual organisation 2
voluntary and statutory organisations 77

walk *see* steps
welfare 103–4; institutions 2; practitioners 1; managers 1; structures 2; system 104
well-being 107; of families 135; and health promotion 147
West London Project 8–9
women 122
working together 121–32, 148; *see also* collaboration